THE EAST GERMAN RISING

THE
EAST GERMAN
RISING

17TH JUNE 1953

Stefan Brant

WITH A FOREWORD BY

JOHN HYND, M. P.

THAMES AND HUDSON

London

Translated and adapted by
CHARLES WHEELER
The original German edition was published by
Steingrüben Verlag, Stuttgart
under the title
Der Aufstand

[1955]

CONTENTS

ILLUSTRATIONS

FOREWORD

by JOHN HYND, *M.P.*

IN 1945 THE VICTORIOUS ALLIED ARMIES EMBRACED EACH other in Berlin. The German War was over. Now, together, we could settle once and for all this delinquent nation that had twice in our lifetime destroyed the peace of our world. Germany lay helpless in her smoking ruins, her Nazis and militarists destroyed or dispersed, her best elements emerging from their thirteen years of concentration camps or exile. With them we would begin to build a new democratic Germany, which in a world at last united in the common task of peaceful re-construction could no longer of itself become a menace to our common security.

That was the picture; that was the hope. It was soon dispel-led—but this time not by Germany. Quadripartite control of Germany failed, because the Russians preferred to create a Communist satellite State in their occupation zone.

How successful have the Russians been? For several years the hundreds of thousands of refugees pouring over to the West in spite of checks and risks brought stories of terror and priva-tion—stories which might or might not in each case be reliable. The refugees gave part of the answer, but were they only mal-contents? How could one ever know, since the expression of open mass opposition in a totalitarian country was, we knew —or thought we knew—impossible.

Not all Germans favoured Hitler; nor all Spaniards Franco; all Poles are certainly not fervent disciples of Stalin. But had the events of July 1944 in Nazi Germany not shown the

9

impossibility of any effective internal revolt against a well-established Police State?

It is in the light of such considerations that the astonishing uprising in Eastern Germany in June, 1953, takes on an historic significance, not only in its immediate impact on a world so long used to regarding totalitarianism, once imposed, as spelling the death of every democratic impulse or action, but in its exposure of the real insecurity of Communism in the satellite countries, if not—as well may be—in Russia itself. Until this event each one of the modern dictatorships had seemed firmly established, and any manifestation of weakness at the very base of their imposing pyramid of power—the masses—seemed impossible. Not that we have been lacking in *reports* of disaffection; of isolated strikes such as those at the Vorkuta Camp in Siberia, or the Barcelona Strikes of 1951, but always the accompanying picture has been one of hopeless isolation, ending in apparent cowed submission.

Almost countless books have been written by individuals who have suffered and subsequently escaped from the Communist countries: the record of the destruction of human rights and freedom; the misuse of trade unions for the purpose of subjecting instead of protecting the worker; the humiliation of the Church and Clergy; the kidnappings and the incarcerations without charge or trial of men and women whose only crime has been a whispered criticism of intolerable conditions—all this is now almost commonplace. A shrug of the shoulders and a murmured "shocking", and one lays down one book to pick up another which, in different language, repeats the same story with an almost monotonous sameness.

The difference with this book is that the events it describes took place, so to speak, on our own democratic doorstep, before the eyes of the world. They have been recorded in part in Press and Film; the pitiful "People's Police", helpless until saved by the Russian tanks, the tearing down of the Communist banner from the Brandenburg Gate under the very machine-guns of the Russians; the marching crowds of workers; the burnings of Communist newspapers and kiosks, and the stoning of Russian tanks. But even the Press and Film cameras could not record the whole breadth of the scene, which stretched far beyond the fringes of Western Berlin into practically every town and village throughout the Eastern Zone of Germany.

What the author recounts is the first full story of this remark-able and quite unprecedented rising of the working people and peasants of a totalitarian country against their oppressors, astounding in its spontaneity and significant in the universal pattern it followed in each sector, however remote, although no plan or co-ordination was possible. Most significant of all, to my mind, is the fact, which emerges from this story, that the first movement of the strikers in each town and village, without exception, was towards the local gaol, to release their comrades and former democratic leaders. Nothing could better illustrate the truth of what we have previously been told or show us more persuasively, where the thoughts and the true allegiance of the workers in such countries lie. Nothing, too, could more con-vincingly prove—what many of us might already have begun to doubt—that even the harshest dictatorship cannot succeed in completely destroying the stuff of which freedom and democracy have been built, the determination of ordinary people, given the slightest opportunity, to throw off their chains and turn on their oppressors. It is, indeed, implicit throughout the history of Man's struggle for freedom, that oppression does not destroy, but only breeds revolt, and sooner or later is forced to concede, as the German and Russian Communists were forced by this uprising to concede, some, at least, of the demands of their protesting victims.

True, the concessions in this case, abject as they were, did not spell Democracy, or Liberty. Such fulfilment rarely follows a single battle, as the Wat Tylers and the Tolpuddle Martyrs in our own history have shown.

The seventeenth of June, too, had its martyrs, the hostages who were duly shot, summarily and without trial or appeal. This, at a time when the Communist Parties and Press in the democratic countries were conducting their frantic campaign against the "brutality" of American Justice in confirming the sentence on the Rosenbergs for High Treason, after years of legal argument, investigation of evidence, appeals to high and still higher Courts. But not a word did these same Communist Parties or newspapers breathe against the monstrous executions in Eastern Berlin where no evidence was even sought or published.

It is the fact that these events and all the evidence are un٬ deniable and so well known to us, that makes this book more intimately real perhaps than any other record yet published of life under Communism. It is probably in the fact that these events are without precedent in any totalitarian country that lies its chief value. Here at last is indisputable evidence that the age٬ old spirit of liberty is not dead.

CHAPTER I

BLUEPRINT FOR RED GERMANY

1945: "Hitlers come and Hitlers go..." ⁄ Proconsul Zhukov ⁄ Deadly embrace: Socialists and Communists unite ⁄ First election ⁄ Colonel Tulpanov and the bourgeois Parties ⁄ Dawn of cold revolution: land reform, nationalisation and class warfare ⁄ The Soviet⁄German Republic is born

THE ROMAN CHARIOT CROWNING THE BRANDENBURG GATE had vanished in the rubble below. A red flag had taken its place. Unter den Linden was deserted, except for two soldiers erecting a sign⁄board outside the scarred shell that was once the Café Kranzler. Framed in red and in big black letters on a white ground, the notice proclaimed: "Hitlers come and Hitlers go—the German people lives for ever. J. V. Stalin." It was one of many such sign⁄boards. They were springing up everywhere; in Berlin and all the towns that had been occupied a few weeks earlier by the soldiers in strange, flat caps and baggy breeches. Hitler had really gone, and a much⁄decorated Marshal named Zhukov had come to represent the man who had signed this assurance of the German people's longevity. It was June 1945: the Reich was defeated and its eastern and central portions had become the Soviet Zone of Germany.

Marshal Zhukov had made his headquarters in the East Berlin garden suburb of Karlshorst—a name that was soon to become a by⁄word. His staff, hidden from public view by a tall wooden fence topped with barbed wire, had established themselves quickly. In the West, Britain, France and the United States had created similar institutions and were ready to tackle

13

the business of occupation. But none could match the speed and precision with which the Soviet Military Administration applied its plans. The Russian officers had come equipped with blueprints, and in the summer of 1945 they embarked on the immense task of re-laying the foundations of the political, economic and social structure of a quarter of Germany.

One of Marshal Zhukov's first ordinances provided for the re-birth of trades unions and a number of "anti-fascist" political parties. His reservation that their activities would be controlled was not unreasonable; to allow unrestricted political activity after twelve years of dictatorship would be to take an unjusti-fiable risk. One political party was spared this mistrust, how-ever—a party whose leaders had stepped from a Russian military Dakota airliner a few days after the fall of Berlin; the German Communist party (KPD) had returned to German soil. The former exiles celebrated their homecoming with a declara-tion of policy firmly rejecting the idea that the Soviet system of government might be imposed upon Germany: "current trends", they explained, demanded the creation of "an anti-fascist democratic order and parliamentary democracy based on the political freedom of the individual". The Soviet Military Governor's early ordinances were no less liberal in tone; Marshal Zhukov seemed to be steering towards a purified form of the old Weimar Republic.

No one was deceived for long, however. Lenin had had to wait in vain for the German revolution and today, twenty-seven years later, his successors were in a position to fashion "current trends" at will.

The Russians knew that their German policy could not suc-ceed without the formal support of at least part of the population. A realistic assessment of public opinion told them that their single ally, the Communist Party, was unloved and that the immensely stronger Social Democratic Party (SPD) would never support the introduction of Communism. It was decided at Karlshorst that the SPD must be sacrificed. The rôle at the altar was assigned to the KPD.

Years of political schooling in Moscow had impressed upon the comrades the lesson that Hitler's rapid ascendancy in Germany was in no small part due to the bitter rivalries among the left-wing parties of the nineteen-twenties and early 'thirties: now it was their turn to teach. The argument was not ineffective, and soon a joint committee of the two parties was preparing for co-operation. But there was no mention of fusion and, when the Russian political advisers and German Communists first made such a suggestion nearly a year later, it was decisively rejected by those Social Democrats who were in a position to do so. In March 1946, eighty per cent of SPD members in Berlin confirmed the stand taken by all but a handful of the party's leaders and voted "No" to the KPD's proposal. But people who concluded that the plan had failed were under-estimating the matchmakers at Karlshorst: the luxury of a ballot was denied SPD members in the Soviet Zone and within a month the merger was announced. "In the interests of working-class solidarity", KPD and SPD had combined to form a single proletarian movement to be called the Socialist Unity Party (SED). The instrument of his own party's liquidation was signed by a prominent Social Democrat named Otto Grotewohl; he was soon to become Prime Minister.

Marshal Zhukov had reserved the right to intervene in the affairs of the young political parties if, in his view, the interests of the occupying Power required protection. And very soon, this *was* his view. With the SPD's downfall, the job of op/ posing the encroachment of Communism passed to the "bour/ geois" parties, the Christian Democratic Union (CDU) and the Liberal Democratic Party (LDP). The CDU in particu/ lar was in constant trouble with the Marshal's political adviser, Colonel Tulpanov. Before the CDU was six months old its joint leaders, Dr. Andreas Hermes and Dr. Walter Schreiber, had been recalled from their posts; they had spoken up in favour of compensation for those dispossessed by land reform. Their successors, Jacob Kaiser and Ernst Lemmer, were no more fortunate: they told Colonel Tulpanov that the Christian De/ mocrats could never recognise as permanent Germany's new eastern frontier along the Oder and Neisse rivers—and their election to the party's executive committee was declared invalid.

The Liberal Democrats fared no better. The "anti/fascist new order" was taking shape and opposition to the Soviet plan for Germany had become virtually illegal. Elections to five pro/ vincial parliaments in the autumn of 1946 were not free: a number of CDU and LDP candidates were arrested by the Russian authorities and the names of others were simply de/ leted from the ballot lists by local garrison commanders. The SED, whose privileged position in the supply of newsprint, transport and rations had come to be accepted by the other parties as inevitable, emerged as the strongest single party and with a narrow majority over its bourgeois rivals.

Moscow's plans for East Germany's transformation were based on land reform, nationalising the means of production and the re/fashioning of the legal system on Soviet lines. No realist questioned the need for the first of the three measures. However, the Russians were moved less by economic than by political considerations: land reform was but a first step towards the introduction of the system of neo-serfdom known to Communists as the collectivisation of agriculture. Accordingly, all owners of more than 250 acres of land were summarily dispossessed without compensation and made to leave the district in which they had "exploited" labour. A little over half the land which thus became available was redistributed to former farm labourers, to "expellees" from former German territory beyond the Oder and Neisse rivers and from neighbouring countries, and to industrial workers and craftsmen. Most of the remainder was used to increase existing small-holdings and to create new "State farms".

Although the immediate consequence of land reform was a fall in agricultural production, the so-called "new farmers" were well satisfied with their property-owning status. They learned the true nature of Moscow's gift to the underprivileged "worker-peasant", however, when a series of laws and decrees began to whittle away their new-found independence. Production plans were now drawn up at Karlshorst. Instructions about times and methods of sowing and harvesting were issued as Military Government ordinances; each farmer was given an individual delivery quota, the size of which was decided in Berlin without regard to local circumstances. Enforcement of delivery was the responsibility of the district administration—in practice, of the SED, which had quickly dominated all levels of local government. Such imponderables as the weather or livestock disease had no part in official calculation. Farmers who, through lack of seed, fertiliser, implements or machinery, were unable to deliver the prescribed amount of produce on time were warned. If, after a period that seldom exceeded ten days, the required amount was still outstanding they were prosecuted in the courts.

Just as land reform was a step towards subsequent collectivi- sation, so the nationalisation of industry was part of a long- term plan to create a planned economy on the Stalinist model which would lend itself to smooth assimilation into the eco- nomic system of the Eastern bloc. But the dominant factor in Soviet economic policy during first years of the occupation was the extraction of reparations. The Russian dismantling teams arrived in Germany hard on the heels of the fighting troops, and they worked with enthusiasm for three years. In October 1945, Marshal Zhukov issued his celebrated Ordi- nance No. 124: "Concerning the requisition and provisional appropriation of certain undertakings in Germany". The order provided for the sequestration of property owned by Nazis and Nazi sympathisers. In fact, the decree was applied quite arbi- trarily. The concerns affected were divided into three groups. Group I consisted of firms whose nationalisation was to be "approved" by popular vote. A dubious form of referendum was indeed held in Saxony and, after the people of this pro- vince had said "yes", the decision was enforced throughout the Soviet Zone without further democratic ado. A second group concerned companies which were to be taken over temporarily; Group III listed concerns in which the occupation power was itself interested. Under this last heading, 213 of the Russian Zone's principal industrial undertakings became Soviet pro- perty. Known as Soviet Corporations (SAG), these produced a third of Eastern Germany's total industrial output.

In modern democracies, independence of the judiciary has come to be regarded as a fundamental principle of the civilized community; in Eastern Germany, the administration of justice was from the earliest days of Russian occupation a means to a political end. Denazification laws—rigorously applied to exclude even nominal Nazis in minor positions—had left an enormous gap in the legal profession, and brief courses in the essentials of jurisprudence were instituted to train judges in the shortest possible time to administer the law according to the Soviet conception of justice as an instrument of political power in the hands of the State. With control of the training courses and the selection of candidates in the hands of the SED, the "people's" justice flourished. "Saboteurs" and "agents" were made responsible for official error and administrative breakdown; opponents of the regime were "unmasked as Fascists and reactionaries" and vanished into overcrowded gaols and concentration camps built by Hitler.

New laws created new offences. The law for the "Protection of the People's Property" and the law for the "Protection of Internal Trade" were economic measures in little more than name. A Leipzig court sentenced a doctor to five and a half years hard labour for breaking the law for the safeguarding of internal trade by buying in the Western sectors of Berlin drugs which he could not obtain in the Soviet Zone. The charge conceded that the accused had "helped very many patients", but added: "In the opinion of the working people, the struggle for German reunification and for the conclusion of a fair peace treaty must take precedence over the interests of individual citizens of the Republic. The defendant's attitude while awaiting trial has shown that he gravely under-estimates the extent of our economic recovery." Similarly, the law for the "Protection of Peace" and the law against "Incitement to War, Murder and Non-coöperation" provided a convenient framework for an unbroken succession of show trials. Another Leipzig court found "incitement to non-coöperation" in the outburst of a village mayor who had told a group of party officials: "Nothing you say has the slightest effect on me. You are building on sand, and sooner or later your system will collapse. There is only one truth, and that is the teaching of Christ."

The doctor, the mayor—or a Potsdam worker who was given eight years hard labour for amending a placard "Out with the Americans" to read "Out with the Russians"—these were but three of many victims of what the Communists called "democratic legality" and class justice. Not only did the courts avenge every slightest sigh of political opposition, they invariably imposed the maximum sentences provided by the law. Acquittals were rare and fines uncommon. In a single year, 51,596 defendants were awarded a total of over 50,000 years of imprisonment while 10,114 people were put behind bars for a total of 30,000 years.

CHAPTER II

THE MONSTER PLAN

The Plan expects... ⁄ The unknown factor X ⁄ Nationalised black market ⁄ Soviet wages policy: exploitation by instalments ⁄ Activists, Norms and Heroism of Labour ⁄ The Trade Union as weapon of State ⁄ Two Year Plan and Five Year Plan ⁄ Collective wages contracts ⁄ Resistance ⁄ Equal rights for women

SCARCELY HAD THE EIGHTEEN MILLIONS BEGUN TO LIVE again than the same dreary regimentation as before set in. The search for a handful of potatoes, for a few books, for a home, a wife, a missing child—every detail of the struggle to build up life once more was dominated by the Plan.

Their teachers in Moscow had taught the German comrades that it is better to organise life than to live. They had learned that only a fool cares about the happiness of the moment and to think of today as no more than the inevitable stepping⁄stone to tomorrow. To the servant of the god who is not primarily concerned with sacrifices of lambs and bread or libations of blood and wine, but to whom is offered up ton upon ton of paper, life always begins tomorrow. Of what account the gasps of the exhausted, the curses of the foot⁄sore, the silence of the dead, if far ahead the Plan lights up in magic brilliance to show the way to Progress? Who among the dazzled masses shall question the road if, as the caravan of subject peoples drags on through the weary years, the mirage ever retreats and tomorrow never comes? Who shall care? The high priests of the Plan drive in well⁄upholstered limousines and allow no pause for rest. They say: Two Years. They say: Five Years. They lay down fixed terms and the succession of terms never ends. They cannot understand that some want to halt a while, to catch their breath, to eat or drink, or dream. They cannot understand that others want to stop—to build a house, be happy, to enjoy the moment. To the planners the urge to change step, to leave the column of route, to be alone, is incomprehensible; for they cannot stop themselves. They demand progress in unison, and insist that privacy is wrong. The Plan is everything, or nothing. It dominates field and bedroom, workshop and crèche, barrackroom and family hearth. The Plan forbids the unexpected; for it expects. The Plan excludes the unpredictable; it predicts.

Yet the unexpected does happen. Life is not a machine nor is man a robot. Nature defends itself and takes its revenge. Freedom can never be wholly stifled. The Plan makes no provision for failure, weakness, anger, humour, willingness and unwillingness. It ignores the unknown factor, X. X equals strength and weakness, success and failure, joy and sorrow, obedience and refusal. X is the individual, the ego multiplied by millions —perplexing because it is free. X is freedom and, when freedom is suppressed, X can equal violence.

Life cannot be reduced to utilitarian function. Life does not glide along the rails the Plan provides. The people at the schoolroom desk of the total Planners' State think out of turn and are not to be cured of it. If they do not want to march, they break ranks—and either bolt or collapse. The planners call them "expendable". But the account no longer balances: 100 per cent minus expendability no longer equals 100 per cent.

Man is not material to be hammered, anealed, moulded, cast and used at will. And man in his weakness is still strong enough to corrupt the material upon which the planners think they can rely. The factor X in man, the producer, crops up again as factor X in the product. They build a hundred locomotives. Twenty-five fail to pass the test: "Expendable!" They make a thousand electric light bulbs. Two hundred and fifty fail after two hours' burning: "Expendable!" Quantity at the price of quality. Faulty planning, faulty organisation, faulty production...... The Plan reigns but perversity snaps at its heels. The Plan asks for the product; it never asks after the producer. Man is the means; he is never the end. So achievement lags behind. The Plan demands greater effort. Still man is but the means. And still achievement lags. The system fails.

True, it can point to imposing successes. It was the Plan's dictatorship which transformed the Soviet Union into a mighty industrial power in two decades. It was the Plan which forged powerful new industries in Poland, Czechoslovakia and Eastern Germany. It has often attained the seemingly impossible. Yet it has failed. It has never achieved its end. It has changed the world but not Man; it has transformed conditions of life but not life itself. The Plan has never conquered the individual. It has failed to uproot the unknown factor, X.

The victor exercised his rights. He demolished, dismantled and carried off to his own land giant factories with the pick of their staffs. The bulk of the remainder he declared "people's" or Soviet property and put party members, distinguished for ideological rather than technical ability, in the directors' chairs. The people went to work among the ruins. In the factories, the few qualified men who had survived fighting, capture and subsequent waves of arrest and deportation were joined at the lathes and benches by refugees from the eastern territories, clerks and civil servants, farmers and, above all, by women whose husbands were dead, captured or simply missing. Their object was the same—to earn a little money and a higher grade of ration card.

In 1948 the government founded the "State Trading Organ⁄isation" or H.O.—a chain of stores offering food off the ration at an inflated price. In the H.O. shops those who could afford it might buy a pound of margarine for 25 marks—a sum which it took the unskilled labourer five days to earn—a pound of butter for 35 marks, or a pound of flour for 4 marks. It was an effective system and, although the prices ruled out the regular patronage of the ordinary mortal, the State's own legalised black market earned a revenue of thousands of millions of marks.

According to the percentages issued by the official statisti⁄cians, the standard of living was rising appreciably year by year. In fact, the eighteen millions were straining to reach what their more fortunate countrymen across the River Elbe regarded as a bare subsistence level. It was sheer hunger that forced them to spend on food in the H.O. stores money which, under a more equitable system of distribution, would have gone to replace tattered underclothes, worn⁄out shoes, broken furniture and missing pots and pans.

There was no alternative; they had to eat. But if there was ever again to be a tolerable standard of living, then either prices must fall or wages rise.

In the event, the Communists chose to raise wages—in their own inimitable style. Stalinist dogma condemned "dreary equality" as "unsocialistic", and the German Marxists adopted a system of grades so radical in its divisions as to make the most cruel of capitalists blush. While the unskilled workman in the electrical industry was taking home a weekly wage of less than

£ 3, the official gazette announced that highly qualified technicians would be paid weekly salaries of £ 75, and "certain
specialists" no less than £ 290 a week. And the higher the
salary, the higher the food ration: while the factory worker paid
twelve shillings for a cooked sausage in the H.O. store, his
works manager drew, in exchange for a token sum of money,
an "intelligentsia parcel" containing, among other food, eight
pounds of fresh meat. As an additional incentive, the Government instituted special shops in which the privileged classes
could buy at remarkably reasonable prices the clothing and
consumer goods which the working man could neither find
nor afford.

In the factories, the Party taught that exploitation had been
abolished and that wages now depended upon productivity.
And in 1948 the government presented the industrial worker
with the equivalent of the farmer's delivery quota—the "technically substantiated norm".

The use of the individual norm in calculating wages was not
unknown. In earlier times, each man's norm—or the amount
of work required of him in a given time—had been assessed on
the basis of the *average* output of all his work-mates. The required amount of work secured him his basic wage, and his
output in excess of the norm was rewarded accordingly. The
S.E.D. condemned this system as "infamous, outmoded and
capitalistic", and represented the new method of calculation
as something quite different. It was, indeed. The new norm
was "technically substantiated"—it was defined as "the amount
a man is able to produce in a given time if he makes the best
possible use of the tools and materials at his disposal". The
"socialistic" norm was an improvement on its "capitalistic"

predecessor in that it demanded not average but maximum performance. Before long the "norms commissions" moved into
the factories and the experts on other people's productivity took
up their positions alongside the lathes and presses, stop-watch
and notebook in hand.

"Heroism of Labour" had arrived. On October 13, 1948
the face worker, Adolf Hennecke, of the "Karl Liebknecht"
coalmine "fulfilled his norm with 380 per cent"—or cut his
required quota of coal as well as nearly twice the amount be-
sides. It was an astounding performance. But before his work-
mates had had time to express their admiration, the story spread
that a year earlier Hennecke had attended the SED's political
academy at Meerane—and had written his thesis on "Stakha-
nov, a Soviet example to the German worker". Hennecke had
been fed, trained and fostered like a champion boxer for the
great day. Afterwards, he toured the mines and factories of the
Republic, became star speaker at party and trades union rallies,
was rewarded with the "National Prize, First Class" (a medal
and £ 8,000 in cash)—and finally disappeared from view
under an avalanche of paper at the desk of a departmental chief
in the Ministry of Heavy Industry.

At first it seemed a joke. Hennecke-stories were bandied
about everywhere: the great man had dropped his pay packet
on his foot, which had then to be amputated; he had divorced
his wife for refusing to effect in three months a process not normally completed in less than nine. But Hennecke had brought
the Stakhanovite movement to Germany and his accomplish-
ment quickly found its imitators. The "activists" multiplied
like rabbits. The Leipzig engine-driver, Heine, developed the
"500 movement" (every locomotive to be driven 500 kilo-

metres a day); a truck driver began the "100,000 movement" (each vehicle to clock 100,000 kilometres without a general overhaul); a "4,000 litre movement" committed the cows to an annual output of 4,000 litres of milk. Following the example of the Soviet National Prizewinner, Chutkich, the weaver Striemann of Cottbus served a dozen looms simultaneously. Factory shifts were organised into "Brigades" and, when the near-hysterical demand for quantity threatened to undermine the last remnants of craftsmanship, fame and honour were be-stowed upon "Brigades of Excellent Quality", the first of which was formed by Louise Ermisch of the People's Own Clothing Factory at Halle. With the cash prize as a bribe, the activists' movement breached the workers' tradition of solida-rity. "Socialist competitions" followed: factories publicly chal-lenged one another in quarterly races for a bonus and a banner to increase production, save materials and lower costs.

The propaganda display which accompanied the introduc-tion of Russian industrial methods has scarcely diminished to-day. The party agitators banged their drums in strict Soviet time and piped the Russian tune without pausing to consider whether a publicity campaign which had proved successful in the young industrial State to the east could be applied with equal effect in Germany, a modern industrial nation with a strong tradition of technical achievement and high quality production. What of the trades union movement, guardian of the working man's rights and his protector from exploitation? In 1946, the Soviet Zone "Free German Trades Union Feder-ation" (FDGB) had three million members and its leadership was allotted a modest rôle in the affairs of state. Insofar as it was permitted at all, the day-to-day work of the unions was the responsibility of the Works' Councils, bodies that were largely manned by old trades unionists of the pre-Nazi period. The Communists' early attempt to infiltrate into the councils had misfired and the Government was compelled to adopt more direct methods. The FDGB set up parallel organisations in each factory and, in 1948, a Government decree granted the FDGB the exclusive right of representation. The trades union official's job was now to represent not the worker but the Party; he was to popularise the norms, collect "voluntary under-takings" to raise output, and supervise factory discipline.

The "Two Year Plan", launched on New Year's Day, 1949, with the limited objective of restoring production to the 1938 level, was succeeded in 1951 by a mightier monster. The "Five Year Plan" embraced the administration, finance, agriculture, education, sport, "culture" and, above all, industry. By the end of 1955, industrial production was to exceed the 1950 level by 92.3 per cent. Priority was given to heavy industry—as in Prague, Warsaw, Budapest, Bucharest and Sofia, the planners were obliged to submit to the overall Plan of the Soviet system, taking orders from the "State Planning Commission" (*Gosplan*) in Moscow.

And so began the headlong expansion of heavy industry which was to carry Eastern Germany's economy to the brink of ruin within two and a half years. Without a thought for the day-to-day needs of the population, for the post-war plight of industry or for the interdependence of the Eastern and Western German economies, the Five Year Planners decreed the expan-sion of the metals industry by 153.6 per cent, of the machine tools industry by 114.8 per cent and of the chemicals industry by 104.4 per cent. A continual rise in productivity was taken for granted from the outset, and each nationalised or Soviet-owned factory was allotted its individual plan and its individual wages budget. During the next five years, the worker's right to demand more pay disappeared with his right to change his job. Instead, he was given the "collective wages agreement".

Introduced in the name of progress as a triangular contract between State, factory and worker, the new agreement invited the industrial employee to accept as irrevocable both targets and wage rates as laid down in the Five Year Plan. Party and trades union officials were schooled and, armed with draft contracts and the latest red and yellow issue of "Notes for the Agitator", were sent into the workshop to acquaint the under-privileged proletarian with the latest gift from the Soviet Union. But the victims declined to be enlightened; not without logic, they pointed out that contracts required acceptance—and re-jected them. The argument continued for months. Second drafts were prepared and again many of the large factories re-fused them. The Government won in the end, but not without a major struggle. The enforcement of the collective wages agreement occupied the party leaders for eleven months—for the first time the SED encountered genuine resistance.

Each year the Plan ate more deeply into everyday life. Sullenly the working people wrestled with the Party for minor, long-established rights. They gained limited successes, as over sickness benefits and in compelling the State to allow working women to keep their free week-day for domestic purposes.

The Communists had granted "equal rights for women"; what they understood by equal rights was made clear in the Labour Law which charged the authorities with "the provision of conditions enabling women to exercise their right to employment in all sectors of the national economy". The Prime Minister, Otto Grotewohl, was more precise when he announced in 1950 that women who were registered with the employment exchanges as unfit for work constituted the last untapped reserve of labour in the Soviet Zone. By 1952 women provided 37.3 per cent of the Soviet Zone's total labour force —the Five Year Plan imposed a target of 40.8 per cent. While women earned equal pay for equal work, a "Law to safeguard Motherhood" cancelled paid holidays before and after confinement. Regulations preventing the employment of women underground and on night-shift were quietly cancelled. Women appeared on scaffolding as bricklayers, worked as deck-hands in trawlers and in a variety of masculine occupations in factories, rolling-mills, shipyards, pits, the railways and the police-force. Short rations and astronomic H.O. food prices provided the incentive. "Equal rights" meant heavy labour for women as for men. It meant separation from children—who were to be brought up by the State in crèches—and the transformation of the family into a "working brigade".

The monster Plan inched its way forward, seeking to destroy even the intimacies of private life. The power of shortage and the dictatorship of Labour drained life of its colour. Faces, clothes and streets became a uniform grey. A godless and desolate Puritanism laid down the law of "Socialist morals", as though Eros himself were being persecuted. Certainly he was driven out of the arts; novels, plays, films and paintings created new heroes of labour, war, revolution and ideology. Laughter died away and happiness disappeared. Years passed before both returned—for a single day, on June 17, 1953.

CHAPTER III

"THE CONSTRUCTION OF SOCIALISM"

"Emergency" at the border ⁄ Self⁄imposed siege ⁄ The Party Confer⁄ence: class warfare is declared ⁄ Socialism in the country⁄side: kulaks and collectivisation ⁄ The farmers' exodus ⁄ The cult of youth ⁄ State versus Church ⁄ The Christian Youth Groups ⁄ Rearmament in public ⁄ Purge of the bourgeois fellow⁄travellers ⁄ Economic break⁄down ⁄ No food for the middle class

THE TOTALITARIAN STATE DEPENDS FOR ITS EXISTENCE on the efficiency of its political police—and upon the isolation of its people. If "tomorrow" is ever to come, then the popula⁄tion must be denied the opportunity to exchange information and make comparisons with its neighbours. It is a rule that ap⁄plies with particular force to the totalitarian state of Eastern Germany, the result of an unnatural division that cuts across nationality, language, history, culture, customs and countless bonds of personal relationships. In the spring of 1952, Eastern Germany began a complex operation to sever connections with the Federal Republic in the West. An announcement that frontier police and customs officials had been placed under the authority of the Ministry of State Security (successor to the Gestapo) coincided with a newspaper campaign for "in⁄creased vigilance in the western border districts". The warning was unmistakable; experience under Hitler had taught that such appeals were followed by reports of "provocations". The SED observed the rule and its Secretary⁄General, Walter Ul⁄bricht, referring to the signature in Paris of the European Defence Community treaty, gave notice that "Western military

provocations" would be answered with "scientific exactitude".
The subsequent stages of the ritual followed in quick succession: the Communist Press published letters and petitions appealing for the armed defence of the homeland against the threat
of invasion from the West, and the Government responded
to the supposed popular alarm with a decree announcing
"emergency arrangements" at the border. These provided for a
narrow strip of forbidden territory along the entire length of the
border with Western Germany, and for an adjacent belt of
land, three miles wide, to which entry without a special permit
was prohibited. A few days later the Government ordered the
evacuation from the three-mile belt of all "unreliable inhabitants"—a category which included known or likely opponents
of the regime, refugees from the Eastern territories now under
Polish administration, foreigners, former regular soldiers,
people known to have ties with Western Germany, employers
of labour, craftsmen, shopkeepers, publicans and owners of
large farms. Some fled westward to the Federal Republic while
there was still time, stampeding across the strips of forbidden
land with horses, carts and cattle. Others took the only safe
escape route that now remained, going by train to East Berlin
and crossing from the Soviet sector to the Western sectors of the
city. In May 1952, while the enforced evacuations from the
Soviet Zone border area were taking place, West Berlin's refugee camps filled to overflowing; the number of those seeking
asylum doubled in a month.

The East German Government also did its best to cut communications between the two halves of Berlin. By digging
ditches, erecting fences, barriers, brick walls and barbed wire
entanglements, the Communists reduced the number of open

roads into the city's western sectors from 227 to 47—a measure which eased their own system of police controls considerably. Then, without warning, they cut telephone and tram communications between East and West Berlin. A few days later, entry into the Soviet Zone was forbidden to West Berliners, a measure which caused much hardship among 30,000 town dwellers—many of them unemployed—who owned bungalows and allotments in the country and who now found themselves arbitrarily dispossessed of property, fruit, flowers and vegetables at the beginning of summer.

Meanwhile, in the interior of the Soviet Zone, numerous new regulations gave the State Security Service wide powers to deal with "diversionists, spies and saboteurs", and Prime Minister Grotewohl ordered the courts to administer class justice with the "toughness of steel". A series of well publicised trials showed that prosecutors and judges had understood their instructions. The atmosphere of the besieged fortress, so familiar in other East and Central European countries, descended on the Soviet Zone of Germany like a pall.

In July, 1952 the cream of the corps of "Party functionaries" was summoned to the capital to attend the Second Conference of the SED. The stage managers had set the scene for an historic occasion. The Werner Seelenbinder Hall, built on the site of Berlin's former cattle market, was a jungle of banners, portraits and plants in pots; over the floodlit stage, and all but smothered in red bunting, Marx, Engels, Lenin and Stalin gazed down at the assembled delegates. The timing of the production was superb. At the very time that the President of the Democratic Republic, Wilhelm Pieck, declared the conference open, Federal

Chancellor Adenauer was asking Parliament in Bonn to approve a first reading of the agreements to bring Western Germany into the European community. The first Opposition speaker in Bonn had not yet risen to his feet when, in East Berlin, Walter Ulbricht stepped to the lectern with a 200-page manuscript. For six hours the veteran Communist sermonised in his unattractive Saxon dialect; his speech, though it was written in the style of a ministerial circular, was far from dull. It contained detailed plans for the "construction of Socialism", or the transformation under "conditions of intensified class warfare" of a central-European country into a Bolshevik state. Ulbricht proclaimed a policy of still higher priority for heavy industry, more nationalisation, the virtual liquidation of the middle class and a series of administrative reforms designed to "bring government closer to the people". He also threatened the Church. Finally, he revealed that Eastern Germany was now ripe for the collectivisation of agriculture.

The Party had laid its plans carefully. A few weeks before, a number of "progressive" farmers of both sexes had assembled in East Berlin and had entrained in the "Blue Express" for Moscow. In the Soviet capital they had been courteously welcomed with floral tributes and taken on a lightning tour of chosen collective farms. An elevating picture of happy husbandry met their eyes and, having absorbed the requisite quota of enthusiasm, the delegates returned home—in time to enable Ulbricht to include in his marathon speech the news that three model "producer co-operatives" had been formed in Germany. Ulbricht added that it was clearly the government's duty to support such a valuable initiative. He also said that collectivisation must be "entirely voluntary".

Certainly it all began harmlessly enough. Interested farmers were offered a choice between three types of co-operative. In the first, only the farmer's arable land became common property. In the second, members pooled their arable land, beasts of burden and machinery. The third type involved the common ownership of all land, including pasture and woodland, of all equipment, larger farm buildings and of the bulk of the farmer's livestock.

Entry was to be voluntary, Ulbricht had said. But he had also promised intensified class warfare, and had spoken in menacing tones of the "kulaks", or owners of larger farms. The Party Press leapt to its cue. When the H.O. stores ran out of meat and the "co-op" of butter, the kulaks were held responsible. There was a grave shortage of labour. Fertilisers were nowhere to be found. The "Machinery and Tractor Stations" were short of manpower, fuel and spare parts and could not cope with the demands on their services. But the Planners had planned: under pressure from above, the tax inspectors and "quota enforce-ment officers" turned the screw and drove the farmers mercilessly. Farmers in arrears of delivery found their bank accounts blocked; they were charged with sabotage, tax evasion and an assortment of anti-State activities. Some were dispossessed of all they owned and sentenced to long terms of imprisonment and the State appointed trustees to take over their farms. As "capi-talists", the owners of larger farms were forbidden to join co-operatives; nor were they allowed to sell out. Many gave up a senseless struggle, often abandoning property that had been handed from father to son for generations. There had always been farmers in the West Berlin refugee camps—arrivals had averaged 70 a day—but in the autumn of 1953 the number rose to 200 and 300 daily.

It was to rise still further. The "new" farmers had their troubles too. Land reform had given them land but very little else. Lack of livestock, machinery, buildings and experience had handicapped them from the start and few had managed to build up a going concern. Nor were they exempt from the back-breaking delivery quotas. And now, after less than half a dozen years of ownership, they were being pressed into what looked like a return to serfdom. Perhaps inevitably, the least efficient were first to join the new collectives. Others followed suit; but the vast majority held back. Pressure increased—and so did resistance. Party speakers organised "foundation meet-ings" in every village. Generally these functions were ignored or sparsely attended; often the speakers were shouted down; sometimes they were forced to withdraw in haste. The SED newspaper, *Neues Deutschland*, complaining of apathy among party officials, reported a case at Friedrichsaue, where members of the embryo co-operative "Ernst Thaelmann" had arranged to meet at the village inn to draw up a constitution. On their arrival the foundation members were chased from the inn by "reactionaries". The meeting adjourned to a private house, where it failed to make progress because the Mayor and village Party Secretary had ignored invitations to attend. Two of the would-be founders quarrelled. There was a fight. A week later, the District Secretary of the SED called the villagers to a public meeting. Again rioting broke out, and he declared the co-operative as "not constituted". The SED organ added that the Mayor and four farmers had been arrested and the village and district secretaries relieved of their posts. But the farmer's life of relative isolation ruled out effective long-term resistance and in four months 2,000 co-operative farms were established.

Six months later the total reached 5,000. The regime, however, paid a steep price for its introduction of Soviet-type agriculture—from January 1952 to April 1952 no less than 22,852 farmers had exchanged home and livelihood under Communism for a straw mattress and six square feet of floor space in a West Berlin camp.

No matter how prosperous, no country could shoulder the burden of a farmers' exodus for long. And this was a country whose people had been living on short rations for a decade. Where the Plan is supreme, however, common sense is sacrificed. Emergency collections of seed potatoes and grain by the "Young Pioneers" merely aggravated the food shortage. Nor did the government's outbursts against the "conscious sabotage of the kulaks", or the show trials and the sentences of hard labour, serve as a substitute for bread and meat. The people, among them the industrial workers, wanted food to eat. They watched the farmers being driven from the country and saw that the next harvest was likely to rot.

By April 1953—with several lean months to go before the harvest festival—the Soviet Zone had reached the end of its potato reserves. For a few brief weeks there was a glut of pork; the shortage of fodder had forced the farmers to slaughter their pigs. But soon even the H.O. stores were without meat and fats, and discomfort became acute distress.

In December 1952, West Berlin took in 11,528 refugees. In January 1953 over 22,396 arrived; in February 31,613; in March 58,605. The flow eased a little in the spring; the total fell to 36,695 in April and to 35,484 in May. To hutted camps, disused factories, air-raid shelters, exhibition halls and private houses—month after month they came, a seemingly endless stream of miserable victims of so-called Socialism.

The Communists were unmoved. They were proud that government and economy in Eastern Germany now bore little resemblance to what they considered to be the out-dated forms of the West. The people, on the other hand, had not only remained "Western" in outlook, they had become less "progressive" with every reform. The Second Party Congress took note of this state of affairs and resolved to pay greater attention to the "struggle for the soul of the people"—in particular of the younger generation.

It was a field in which a massive effort of indoctrination had borne wretchedly limited results. Defeat had found German youth intellectually flexible and ready to grasp at anything new. But the first faint and hesitant cheers at liberation from Nazis and war were smothered by the advancing Red Army in a wave of destruction, looting and rape—and the victor's first chance had gone. The early, relatively liberal months of occupation had shown, however, that not all was irretrievably lost. It was a time of intensive discussion, in which the slogan "anti-Fascism" had a big appeal among a younger generation disillusioned by defeat. The controllers at Karlshort, had they troubled to watch, might have noticed a strong inclination towards Socialism. But anti-Fascism, as practiced by the victor, became synonymous with Communism and many crimes were committed in its name. The hungry young Germans were speaking of social democracy—and meant freedom.

It is not impossible that many of them, in their confused desire for social justice, would have eventually accepted the Communist blandishments. But Karlshorst shied away from dangerous experiments. Instead of allowing the young people to mature intellectually, the Russians offered Communism—

heavily laced with material attractions. The Free German Youth (FDJ) monopolised sport and provided walking tours, camp-fire songs and "healthy, organised competition". It sought to capture adolescent ambition and energy by providing a flurry of activity which served as a substitute for "belief" because it filled the day. Without the slightest inhibition, the Party pursued the cult of Youth as Hitler had done. It spent millions in order that a hundred thousand children might have the thrill of marching under a sea of flags. Nineteen-year-olds were made Mayors and twenty-four-year-olds, Ministers of Education. Boys were placed in charge of trams and trains, and the term "Youth train" appeared in the footnotes to official time-tables. "Youth-Brigades" entered the Socialist competitions in industry and the regime seized every chance to swathe them in honours and decorations. The State offered scholarships, filled the high schools with working-class sons and was never sparing of privileges. The Communists' efforts were not unrewarded. They gained a cadre of blind believers; and they created an army of opportunists and indifferents who swam with the stream as long as the demands on them were not too great. But the Party failed to prevent a strong élite from emigrating mentally to the West, carrying with them the majority of the younger generation. And here the regime was powerless.

It was powerless above all against religion. The Party was unable to prevent the Christian churches from offering relief from spiritual chaos. It was compelled to tolerate the eager response of tens of thousands and to watch the Christian communities—instead of withdrawing into a ghetto of convenient mental retreat—turning to the world about them and taking up the struggle against hunger, cold and loneliness. The Com-

rades watched and waited. Their orders were to show a friendly
face. Stalin, when his empire was threatened by Hitler's in-
vaders, had unlocked the church doors and had offered the
Orthodox leaders peace. And the Russian Bishops had shown
grateful obedience towards a State that had a thousand times
called God an invention of reactionary criminals, and had as
many times proclaimed the destruction of the Christian faith
as one of the foundations of its policy. Stalin had mobilised the
burning affection of the moujik for Mother Russia by allowing
him to love her soul, the Church, freely and without fear of
punishment. And as a by-product of his cunning experiment,
Stalin had gained a Church subservient to State.

Why should the experiment not succeed in Soviet-occupied
Germany? Only two of the eighteen millions owed allegiance
to the implacable Vatican; there was common cause between
the Communists and the Evangelical Church in the matter
of anti-Fascism; several of the Church leaders showed strong
left-wing tendencies. Moreover, there were the close ties of the
German Evangelical Church with their brother Churches in
Poland and Czechoslovakia... why should the experiment
fail?

The Christian Democratic Union, once its founders had
been forced to depart for the West, provided no insuperable
obstacle. The prescient old ex-journalist, Otto Nuschke, and
his young assistants had made talented approaches towards the
teachings of Marx and Lenin; they even invented a rose-
coloured philosophy known as "Christian Realism". Their
creation flopped, however. It was ignored by the Church, the
laity in general were not interested and the younger members
were openly antagonistic. Before long, Nuschke and his

"Christian" fellow-travellers found themselves isolated; no one took them seriously. The young people—whether they came from religious or "freethinking" families, from the "bourgeois" or the working classes—joined the Church communities in numbers which grew in direct proportion to the demands and pressure of the State. The Church benefited enormously from its rejuvenation; it gained in strength and influence, and it refused to bow.

And so the Communist leaders' attitude of toleration came to an end. At the Second Party Congress, Ulbricht announced: "Under the conditions of an aggravated division of Germany, the Church no longer has the right to hide its sympathies behind a mask of neutrality. The Church of the Democratic German Republic must decisively repudiate all British and American agencies."

Ulbricht's gale warning was not entirely unexpected. For several weeks past, the Free German Youth—following the earlier examples of *Komsomol* in Russia and Hitler Youth at home—had been huffing and puffing at the Christian Youth Groups. At first, the boys and girls with a small silver cross in their button-holes were simply subjected to cheap abuse. These tactics failed to make an impression, however, and after the Party Conference had cleared the way for official action, the authorities took a hand. When in June 1952 some 4,500 youngsters met for a small Church congress at Luebbenau, they were presented by the local authority with a ban on all meetings other than those to be held in churches and church halls, and on their use as dormitories; orders also forbad local families to provide sleeping quarters for more than two guests. They were served, furthermore, with notices, requisitioning meat which the organisers had bought for the purpose of communal feeding. In justification of these measures, the authorities used a legalistic quibble that was to be repeated on countless occasions in the next few months: the Christian Youth Groups were not included in the official register of approved organisations and were consequently "illegal". The contention of the Evangelical bishops that the Christian Youth Groups were not an independent organisation but a part of the Church, made no difference whatever. The State went over to direct persecution. Boys and girls were bullied in classrooms and some were summoned by their headmasters, to be offered a choice, as a rule in front of a Party or police official, between signing an undertaking to withdraw from the Youth Group or expulsion. Some gave in, and no one could blame them. But the overwhelming majority stood firm—two thousand children were expelled in a few weeks.

In July, the Ministry of the Interior declined to grant exit visas to 5,000 clergy and laymen who had applied for permission to attend the conference of the World Lutheran Federation in Hanover. Another 20,000 people were refused permits to travel to Stuttgart for the annual Evangelical Congress. The Evangelical and Catholic bishops in West Berlin, whose jurisdiction extended over large parts of the Soviet Zone, and whose work had not been affected by post-war demarcation lines, were constantly denied entry. Throughout the summer the State increased its pressure—and the churches their membership and strength. Arrests of pastors and prominent laymen began in December 1952; at least fifty churchmen were imprisoned between Christmas and Easter of 1953. But it was the young Christians who bore the brunt of the attack. On April

28, 1953, the Bishop of Berlin and Brandenburg, Dr Dibelius, addressed them in a pastoral letter: 'It now frequently happens that church services are disturbed by the FDJ, that younger children are forbidden to attend divinity lessons in schools, that the Church is deprived of its property, that its servants are arrested. The work of the Youth Groups goes on. I greet those who have remained firm in difficult times. To those from whom signatures have been extorted, I say this: God's forgiveness is greater than human failings. Extorted signatures have no validity in His eyes. God knows that your consciences have every reason to be clear!"

Bishop Dibelius also called on the Attorney-General in East Berlin and laid a charge of libel against the editorial board of the FDJ newspaper, *Young World*, on behalf of the Youth Groups. The Bishop supported his charge with extracts from the East German Constitution relating to freedom of belief and worship. No action was taken and the battle between State and Church went on.

The Communists' campaign against Christian youth was more than an ideological struggle; it had its roots in practical politics. The second Party Conference had called for rearmament. At the opening ceremony, the assembled delegates had been visited by units of the People's Police—with the Senior Service, the "Sea Police", in the place of honour at the head of a column that had marched into the Assembly Hall. President Wilhelm Pieck had then announced the need for a People's Army: the younger generation, he had said, must not only be practised in the art of small-bore shooting, they must acquaint themselves with the military sciences. Pieck had added that there must be no "bourgeois stupidity" about rearmament: "If we are not to fall an easy prey to the Western aggressors, we must follow the example of the victorious Red Army and master the technique of modern warfare on land, at sea and in the air".

The recruiting officers went into the factories, universities and schools. One such visit in Mecklenburg was reported in the Press as follows. "A wave of enthusiasm mounts. Our friends of the People's Police—among them a detachment of Sea Police—marches into the hall. Hand to his cap, the commanding officer reports: 'Night and day we stand on guard for peace! Long live the readiness of German youth to defend the Republic with arms!'"

A despatch from Bad Salzungen appeared in an East Berlin paper: "A delegation of frontier police marched into the room with rifles at the slope. A storm of deafening cheers broke out as four armed police mounted a guard of honour over the Stalin banner—our symbol of defence."

The Party poets went over to the mass production of stirring tributes to "fighting patriotism". One minor laureate immortalised the exhilaration of response to the call to arms in a work entitled *"Departure for the Depôt"*,

> I sing, I sing, I sing;
> The works bids me adieu,
> I take my gun and go on guard
> For you, my lathe, for you!

Notices of individual "voluntary registrations" for "honourable armed service" (the word "military" was reserved for use in references to the West) appeared in the daily papers. A new para-military organisation, the Society for Sport and Technics, provided adolescents with tactical and weapon training, para-chute jumping and a variety of related pursuits; a new labour corps, "Service for Germany", offered 17-year-old volunteers of both sexes the opportunity to live in camps and take part in "the great Socialist construction projects". The recruiting offi-cers redoubled their efforts, and the proportion of young people among those seeking asylum in West Berlin rose from 25 to 40 per cent.

The skeleton army, or "barrack-based police", at this time numbered approximately 60,000—a cadre of officers, N.C.O.s and specialists for a dozen divisions. Only the recruits were missing.

Relentlessly, the SED set the pace of the advance towards "Socialism", sweeping aside all opposition. Yet another of Ulbricht's reforms dissolved the five provincial governments, their parliaments and even the provinces themselves. Fifteen new districts were created in order "to bring government closer to the people" and, dispensing with elections, the SED packed the new administrations with "progressive elements" from its own ranks. Two swift blows were aimed at the bourgeois par-ties, CDU and LDP. Georg Dertinger, a Christian Democrat and Foreign Minister of the Democratic Republic, was arrested for "hostile activities". The Liberal Democrat Minister of Food, Hamann, was made a scapegoat for the appalling food situation and was imprisoned as a "saboteur". The former friends and colleagues of both men hurriedly issued statements praising the State Security Service for its vigilance, and calling on their followers in the bourgeois parties to hurry along the road to Socialism in the wake of the working class.

But the pace of the working class was, at best, a sullen shuffle. The Government's administrative reforms had caused a remarkable breakdown in the supply system. District boundaries changed overnight, local administrations were removed from one town to another and no one was able to define his new areas of responsibility; the transport and distribution services, already strained to the limit by inflexible planning, collapsed in hopeless confusion. In April 1953, the Government resorted to a panic measure which only underlined its own helplessness and complete lack of regard for human suffering. A decree announced the withdrawal of food ration cards from all houseowners, private employers, businessmen and independent tradesmen of all kinds. A second decree raised the prices of offtheration food in the H.O. stores.

The middle class, it seemed, was to starve.

CHAPTER IV

"THE HAIR-PIN-BEND OR 'NEW COURSE'"

Death of Stalin ╱ High Commissioner Semyonov ╱ Soviet policy revised ╱ State bows to Church ╱ The Politbureau recommends… ╱ The great about-turn ╱ Will the Government resign?

ON MARCH 6, 1953, JOSEPH STALIN DIED. THE PEOPLE OF the Soviet Zone and East Berlin received the news quietly, scarcely daring to hope that the dictator's sudden end would change their lot. Six weeks later Vladimir Semyonov, political adviser in the Soviet Control Commission and widely regarded as an exponent of a policy of relative moderation towards the West, was recalled to Moscow. The appointment of his suc-cessor, Pavel Judin, a leading ideologist of the Soviet Com-munist Party and prominent Cominform official, led to speculation in West Berlin. It had become manifest that the construction of Socialism had plunged the Soviet Zone into a grave economic crisis—was Moscow proposing to turn the screw still further? On May 28, however, it was announced that the Red Army had been relieved of its political functions, and Semyonov returned to East Berlin as Soviet High Commissioner.

A fortnight later the swing became apparent. On June 10, Prime Minister Grotewohl invited the Evangelical Church leaders to a discussion with members of the Government. Next day, a communiqué announced that negotiations had resulted in "wide agreement on the restoration of normal relations be-tween State and Church". The State, it continued, was willing to guarantee the Church's independence. There would be no further measures against the Youth Groups and other Church organisations. Children expelled from schools and universities would be readmitted; religious teaching would be resumed. Requisitioned church property would be returned to its former owners, official grants would be paid in full, court sentences passed on the Church's servants would be reviewed and, where necessary, miscarriages of justice set right.

It was a truly sensational event: the totalitarian State had bowed to the Church. Observers noted with interest that in addition to Premier Grotewohl, Vice-Premier Nuschke of the CDU and Minister of State Security Zaisser had taken part in the meeting—that Walter Ulbricht had not.

This was the curtain-raiser to a chain of events which followed one another at remarkable speed. On the following day, the Politbureau of the SED issued the text of a resolution it had adopted on June 9, calling a halt to "Socialism".

"The Politbureau of the Central Committee of the Socialist Unity Party resolves to recommend to the Government of the Democratic Republic the adoption of a series of measures designed to bring about a decisive improvement in the standard of living of all sections of the population and to strengthen the legal rights of individuals. The Politbureau's recommendations are based upon its recognition of a series of errors on the part of the SED and the Government. These have found expression in decrees and ordinances such as those concerning the overhaul of the rationing system, the placing of abandoned farms under trusteeship, the emergency measures for the collection of farm produce, taxes etc. The interests of certain sections of the population such as farmers, independent traders, craftsmen and the intelligentsia have been neglected. In making its

1. LEIPZIG, 1952: "SEA POLICE" PARADING

ERHÖHT DIE BEREITSCHAFT ZUR VERTEIDIGUNG DER HEIMAT
UND ZUM SCHUTZE UNSERER DEMOKRATISCHEN ERRUNGENSCHAFTEN!

2. LEIPZIG, MAY 1953: ARMED FDJ GIRLS

3. BERLIN, JUNE 17: DEMONSTRATORS AT THE BRANDENBURG GATE

recommendations, the Politbureau is mindful of the supreme importance of Germany's reunification, an objective which cannot be realised unless both sides take practical steps to alleviate present divisions.

"For these reasons, the Politbureau proposes a shift of emphasis from heavy industry to the needs of workers, farmers, the intelligentsia and all members of the middle class. In order to increase the supply of consumer goods which can be produced by private enterprise, and in order to extend the system of distribution, it is recommended that generous short-term credits be granted to applicants in a number of branches of private industry and commerce. The coercive measures for the collection of taxes and social security contributions in private industry and commerce shall be rescinded. Requests for permission to resume business from persons who have closed or handed over their concerns are to be granted immediately.

"In the agricultural field, the Politbureau recommends the cancellation of decrees relating to the disposal of abandoned farms and property and to the installation of trustees in cases of arrears of delivery or taxes. Farmers of all categories who have fled to West Berlin or Western Germany because of difficulties in carrying on their work should be offered the opportunity to return to their holdings and should be granted credits in cash and kind. If, in exceptional cases, restoration proves to be impossible, such farmers should be paid compensation in full. All punishments in cases of non-delivery of produce and non-payment of taxes shall be reviewed.

"The Politbureau further recommends that all refugees who choose to return to the territory of the Republic have restored to them property requisitioned under the decree of July 17,

1952. Where, in exceptional cases, this is impossible, they must be compensated. Their flight from the Republic shall not be held against them.

"The Politbureau is of the opinion that the question of entry permits for West Germans and West Berliners, and that of inter-zonal passes for citizens of the Democratic Republic who wish to visit Western Germany, require review in the interests of freer travel. In future, family matters are to be taken into account in granting permits. Particular attention is to be paid to the requirements of scientists and artists wishing to attend conferences in either part of Germany.

"The Politbureau recommends that the Ministry of Justice shall arrange for the immediate discharge, except in serious cases, of prisoners serving sentences of one to three years for offences against the law for the Protection of the People's Property. All persons awaiting trial under the above-mentioned law and who are expected to receive sentences not in excess of this legal minimum of 1-3 years are to be released from custody.

"Finally, the Politbureau recommends that the Government restore food ration cards to all citizens according to the occupational grades provided by the law."

This remarkable document appeared on the front pages of Party newspapers on the morning of June 11 and people rushed to obtain a copy. The Party officials, opening their *Neues Deutschland*, and hoping to find support for their day's task of building up Socialism, were badly shaken. The Comrades rubbed their eyes, whispered excitedly, and cautiously sought the opinion of the District Secretary. But this authority was cursing in a corner. For a brief moment he had wondered whether one of the 'agencies' in West Berlin had succeeded in introducing a forgery into the Party Press.

And yet it was all true. The Politbureau admitted that the rights of the individual required strengthening—hitherto only "diversionists" had suggested such a thing. The Politbureau admitted that Party and Government had made mistakes. They had erred in withdrawing ration cards from house-owners and independent tradesmen, in dispossessing the farmers, in their enforcement of the delivery and taxation regulations. They had been mistaken, too, in pursuing the policy of expanding heavy industry at the expense of the production of consumer goods. But were they not following Stalin's teaching to the letter—that any sacrifice was justified in the creation of a mighty heavy industry? Suddenly everything was wrong. Semyonov had called a halt to progress, and loyalty to the Party line had become personal guilt.

Blow followed blow. Grotewohl ordered the FDJ to call off its abuse of the Youth Groups. A thousand flats, recently requisitioned in Magdeburg, were returned to their owners. Arms production and recruiting were quietly stopped; the People's Police were ordered to abandon weapon training for women and girls; a text-book on pre-military training was withdrawn. No more was heard of the slogan "construction of Socialism". Requisitioned businesses and farms—here and there at least—were actually returned to their rightful owners. Everyone had a right to a ration card and the latest price increases were cancelled. People were allowed to visit relatives in the West, and to receive them. And most important of all, "economic criminals" were released from the prisons. It seemed that the whip had been wrenched from Ulbricht's hand. In the villages and factories of the zone, in the streets of East Berlin, in West Berlin and in Bonn—the question everyone asked was whether the dictator from Saxony could possibly hold on to his position of supremacy. The Comrades wondered uneasily whether Moscow was preparing to expose them to the horror of free elections and German unity: was the Republic no more than a sand castle, able to be demolished as quickly as it had been built? A few sentences in the official Soviet newspaper *Taegliche Rundschau* indicated that the sinners of East Berlin were minor characters in a greater drama: the paper conceded that the Soviet Control Commission was "to a certain extent responsible for recent errors". Moscow, then, was accepting part of the blame. Who in the Kremlin was accusing whom? Had Soviet policy in Germany become the centre of a struggle for power among Stalin's heirs?

The people of Eastern Germany wasted no time in complex speculation. They took note of the fact that the infallible Party had made mistakes and admitted making mistakes. They smiled a little at the memory of the song of praise, "The Party is always right..." They realised that the regime was in retreat. They saw that the petty dictators at town and village level had suddenly lost their voices and were scared of being punished for obeying orders from above. They noticed that Party and administration were suddenly paralysed. For years the people had been humbled, deprived of their rights and forced to hold their tongues—and now the oppressors were bowing to the oppressed. The workers and the farmers raised their heads—cautiously at first, then more confidently. Feeling their way carefully, they followed up the regime's retreat. They began to hope again. Quietly the word went round—perhaps the SED Government would resign. The farmers made their complaints openly and it sounded as though they were making demands. In some towns women assembled at prison gates, calling for the release of their menfolk.

In the churches people offered up prayers of thanksgiving.

CHAPTER V

".....TO LIVE LIKE HUMANS!"

The missing concession · Unrest in industry · "If Marx only knew..." · Trouble on the Stalinallee · The Party Press warns · Of deaf dictators

THE SED, ON INSTRUCTIONS FROM THE SOVIET HIGH commissioner, had made concessions to the weaker, less vocal sections of the community—the farmers and the middle class. Evidently a gesture towards the "proletariat", the industrial working class, was considered unnecessary.

This was surprising; there had been signs of unrest since the beginning of the year when the Government had intensified its campaign for the "voluntary" raising of norms. In fact the Government had had little choice, for its financial policy of keeping prices up while holding wages down had failed to avert a crisis. The demands of heavy industry, the erratic arrival of raw materials, continual power cuts and a variety of obstacles beyond the control of local management had combined to bring about an inflation that threatened to get out of hand. To make up losses of output, the workers had to put in extra hours at higher rates of pay, with the inevitable result that more money chased a declining supply of food and other consumer goods. The regime chose the only remaining method of raising production—it sent the agitators into the factories to press for more work for less pay. But the workers' backs were already bent enough. On the April 28 (six weeks before the proclamation of the "new course") "People's correspondent" Maria Ebeling reported to *Neues Deutschland* from Magdeburg: "The men of the Karl Marx works maintain that they would not be so crazy as to raise their norms". And in Potsdam, the SED's local newspaper complained editorially that "by no means all the workers are fighting with the necessary enthusiasm for the fulfilment of the Plan". In Halle, the newspaper *Freiheit* remarked: "In the mines of this district, trade union leaders are standing by helplessly while output lags behind the Plan. Why? They say they are frightened of asking too much of the miners." The men's resistance, it seemed, was being cautiously supported by at least some officials of the State's own trades union organisation. Reporting the proceedings at a delegate meeting of the Chemical Industries Union, *Freiheit* wrote: "A speaker from the ElectroChemical combine at Bitterfeld spoke against the voluntary raising of norms. His attitude amounted to provocation."

"Provocation" was the cue, and the Party issued a call for "mass vigilance". The hunt for saboteurs was taken up with renewed vigour. That the industrial working class had reached the limit of its endurance—and of its patience—could surely not be true. The Central Office of Statistics announced that the plan for the first quarter of 1953 had "only been fulfilled up to 96 per cent" and that many factories had exceeded the "permitted ratio of wages to output". The Politbureau hesitated no longer. On May 14, the Party's Central Committee adopted a resolution recommending the Government to "secure a general raising of working norms, by an average of ten per cent by June 1". As a rule, the Party's recommendations were confirmed as Government decrees with 48 or 96 hours. But in this case there was a delay of 14 days, and when Grotewohl's Cabinet eventually took active notice of the norms question on

May 28 it was already too late to achieve the scheduled result.

The SED newspaper *Leipziger Volkstimme* had reported trouble among printers in its issue of May 23, reminding its readers that since the turn of the century the printing trade had suffered from the machinations of "opportunists and Social Democrats" who were nothing less than "agents of the bour-geoisie". One such villain was Comrade Tschirpe (SED) who had publicly demanded a return "to the old spirit among printers" and had described loyal Party members as lackeys. Comrade Tschirpe had gone on to criticise the struggle for increased norms, infecting Comrade Ristau, who had permit-ted himself the remark: "All we need is a free election—then the Comrades who are now agitating for higher norms will see what they can do with their Party."

So Party members were daring to show open defiance. On May 29, *Freiheit* printed another of its colourful despatches from the industrial front: "Mates, what's happening here is a disgrace. Seventy years after the death of Karl Marx, we're still discussing our most elementary needs. If Marx only knew, he'd turn in his grave. There can be one proposal only and that is: 'Back to common sense!' " The speaker was an old member of the Labour movement named Wilhelm, an employee of the Soviet-owned hydro-electric machinery works at Zeitz. *Freiheit* pub-lished the report on the day following the SED Central Committee's decision to raise the norms—six weeks later. He had stepped down from his platform to the chant of his mates: "We want to live like humans—that's all we ask."

Magdeburg, Halle, Leipzig, Zeitz—the ripples spread out-wards. On June 2 *Neues Deutschland* reported "a stormy en-counter with reactionary arguments" from the nationalised

foundries at Berlin-Lichtenberg. The mechanic Adolf Scher-
mer had resigned from the branch committee of his union on
the ground that he could no longer support the official norms
policy. He had said: "Let them first lower the prices. What
if I do raise my norm? Will it lower the price of shoes? Not that
we could raise the norms if we tried, with our outdated and
creaking machinery."

Whatever its reasons may have been, the Party Press conceded an extraordinary crop of difficulties. The newspapers
could not, however, admit that strikes had taken place in a
dozen or more factories between April 1 and the proclamation
of the new course on June 11. None was more than a short,
sharp stoppage; none was grave enough to put pressure on the
regime—but the warning that the workers were in an ugly
mood was clear enough.

And yet the danger signals were ignored. When the "new
course" was proclaimed, no one doubted that in this most
explosive issue of all the Government would play for safety.
The workers themselves did not doubt it, the Comrades did
not doubt it, even members of the inner circle regarded per-
sistence in the norms issue as risky and irresponsible.

Wages were to be calculated according to the new norms with
effect from June 30, the Government had announced. But
when, in East Berlin on Friday June 5, the building workers
opened their pay packets they found fewer notes inside than
usual; some men found their wage reduced by a quarter, some
by a third. They not only grumbled, they became mutinous—
particularly the bricklayers and carpenters working on Block
40 in the Stalinallee, Eastern Germany's show housing project

and "first Socialist street". Party and trades union functionaries hurried to the scene to "discuss and enlighten" but the men, though they allowed themselves to be persuaded to go back to work, refused to be pacified.

The building operatives of the Stalinallee earned good wages; the skilled man took home 150, 160 and 170 "East"-marks a week. It was not enough for luxurious living: the H.O. stores charged E.M. 10 for a pound of butter (or did so when butter was available); a litre of milk cost E.M. 2; beef (if there was any) was priced at E.M. 7 a pound. But they managed, and they were well aware that their mates on less important projects earned smaller wages. By next pay-day on June 12, however, the men's wives had had a week to budget on the new wage. The skilled man who had drawn E.M. 150 had now laid no more than E.M. 100 on the kitchen table and the truck driver, who had earned a minimum of E.M. 50 a week, had taken home about E.M. 44. The housewives complained bitterly. And now it was pay-day again.

Before giving the sign for paying out to begin, the building manager addressed the 250 men of "Site C-South". Payment on the basis of the new norms, he announced, had now been agreed with their representatives and the argument had gone on quite long enough. But the worst was to come: wages, he added, would be calculated according to the new rates retro-spectively from June 1.

To the men, who knew that the new rates were not supposed to become effective before June 30, this was sheer robbery. They demanded a mass meeting of all the Stalinallee building wor-kers and, when this was refused, someone used the word "strike". But it had not yet come to that.

Next day, Saturday June 13, the atmosphere on the building sites was electric. There was much cursing, much talk, little work, but no strike. The men were angry, but unsure of themselves. If the Party had at this moment shown its customary determination, the building workers' far from united front might—perhaps—have collapsed. But the "new course" had been proclaimed only two days before, and the Comrades in the Politbureau and in the Government were even more uncertain of themselves than were the building workers. As for the rank and file Party members, these were utterly confused. There was not a sound from Walter Ulbricht: was he, or was he not, in power? Who was to tell them—if possible, in writing —what to do next? Which was the right policy: the tough, or the soft?

Nothing is stronger than centralised government, if the centre is strong. But the centre was weak and the workers felt it to be so.

Monday, June 15. The Party's central newspaper, *Neues Deutschland*, had published a long account of the crisis in the Stalinallee in its Sunday edition. Rudolf Herrnstadt, the paper's Editor-in-Chief, was practising the "new course" as he understood it. His reporters, Siegfried Gruen and Kaethe Stern, had collected a mass of unusual stories from the building sites and Herrnstadt had allowed them to call a spade a spade. "It might have been expected (they wrote) that the signs of discontent among the workers about the norms would have prompted the trades union and Party functionaries in the Stalinallee to consider their own work critically. This has not been the case, however... Early in May, the Bricklayers' Brigade Rocke began work at a new site in the Ostseestrasse. 'I hadn't been here more than 20 minutes', Brigadier Rocke told our reporters, 'when three men from the management arrived to discuss the norms with me. I asked them to wait until my whole Brigade was present; half of them were finishing off a job in the Muehlenstrasse. But I was told that my men had already approved the new norms—that the manager there had the signatures of my mates in his pocket. I answered that this was a barefaced lie, and I was right'...

" 'You won't put what we tell you in your paper!' That is how members of Brigade Zock greeted us. 'We have been arguing with the norms department for months', they said. 'Every week the same muddled calculations. Are we supposed to beg for our pay?' "—And *Neues Deutschland* commented in a leading article: "The Norms department is sadly mistaken if it imagines that it can act with impunity against the interests of the building workers for long."

At Block 40 in the Stalinallee, a trade union official called the men together to approve a vote of thanks to the Government for its announcement of the "new course". Nobody objected; somebody proposed an amendment, however, asking the Government to allow a return to payment according to the old norms and it was approved unanimously. A message arrived from trades union headquarters: the amended resolution was not to be sent off until a senior official had had an opportunity to "explain" the norms question at another meeting. But the men had heard enough of explanations; they elected two of their number to deliver the resolution to Grotewohl and Ulbricht personally.

Tuesday, June 16. The senior official from trades union headquarters arrived to find the men of Block 40 in furious discussion

about an article in that morning's *Tribune*, the newspaper published by his own organisation. The writer had evidently decided it was time to clear up any doubts that his colleagues on
Neues Deutschland might have caused. New course or no new
course, he said in effect, the Government's decision to raise the
norms was irrevocable. The bricklayers and carpenters crowded
round their visitor, waving the offending newspaper in his face.
"What does this mean?" they demanded. The official explained
that *Tribune's* article was not a contribution to a debate but an
order. "It means what it says", he declared. "First work more,
then live better."

His remark swept away the vacillation of several days. The
only remaining course of action suddenly became clear to
everyone: a request had been drawn up for submission to the
Government and two men had been chosen to deliver it. The
two must not go alone—Block 40 would go to the Government
in a body.

CHAPTER VI

THE OUTBREAK

The march begins ⁄ *No admittance for strikers* ⁄ *Minister Selbmann is shouted down* ⁄ *Norms, prices and free elections* ⁄ *General Strike* ⁄ *March through East Berlin* ⁄ *A city simmers* ⁄ *The news spreads*

It is 10 a.m. on June 16 and 300 men from block 40 are moving down the Stalinallee towards the Government building in the centre of the city. One of them carries a hastily painted notice, "We demand a reduction in the norms." On the back the sign proclaims: "In honour of May 1, Block 40 of the Stalinallee has raised the norms by 10 per cent." This has been scored out.

The men on the neighbouring site, 'C⁄South', look up, drop their tools and, with scarcely a word, join the ragged little pro⁄cession. From 'D⁄North' opposite, and from 'F⁄South' the men shin down the scaffolding and run to join the strikers. At 'G⁄South' the men are at first doubtful and a few officials try to hold them back. But the call is irresistible; 'G⁄South' joins in almost to a man.

The traffic squeezes the strikers into some semblance of a marching column—by this time 1,500 to 2,000 strong. At the Alexanderplatz, People's Police watch from a respectful distance. A civilian, SED badge in button⁄hole, moves into the middle of the road... and is brushed aside. On the pave⁄ments, passers⁄by stare. A demonstration? On whose instruc⁄tions? Shouts from the marchers confirm that the impossible is happening—that this is no demonstration on instructions from the Government, but a demonstration *against* the Government.

Some of the bystanders make themselves scarce (this can only end in trouble). Others clap and wave encouragement. A few join the ranks.

Rounding the Alexanderplatz, the column makes a detour, picking up another 600 men from ministerial buildings under construction near the Marx-Engels Platz, and moves on up Unter den Linden, passing the great new Soviet Embassy in silence. Turning into the Wilhelmstrasse, the marchers are confronted by a red BMW saloon car. Two officials climb out and onto the roof, shouting to the strikers to return to the Marx-Engels Platz to "negotiate". A few strikers run forward, drag the men off their perch and push the car aside.

In the square outside the "House of the Ministries" in the Leipzigerstrasse the column breaks up. The police guard, sizing up the situation with commendable speed, vanishes into the main entrance and steel shutters clang into position, securing the doors. The two elected representatives of Block 40 ask to be allowed to deliver their message, but are refused admission.

What now? The crowd, constantly reinforced by new arrivals, shouts for Grotewohl and Ulbricht. "Where are our representatives? Hiding in the cellar! Come out and show yourselves..." A first-floor window opens, somebody recognises Selbmann, Minister of Foundry Construction, and Rau, Minister of Mines. "Come down here!" A pause, and both disappear. A moment later police raise the shutters and carry out an office table: Selbmann appears. A young carpenter jumps up and introduces the Minister, who begins:

"Mates..."

"We aren't your mates!"

"...I'm a working-man too..."

"You've forgotten it years ago. You're a traitor!"

The Minister stretches out his arms: "Look at my hands..."
But he is shouted down. "Your hands are flabby. Get off that
table and fetch Grotewohl and Ulbricht."

Five, ten minutes pass—minutes of fresh indecision—and
then an elderly bricklayer scrambles on to the table. "Mates, I
did five years in a concentration camp under the Nazis. But
I'm not afraid of doing another ten under this lot. If I don't
turn up tomorrow you know where I am." And the former
political prisoner lists the men's demands—reduced norms; reduced prices; immunity from punishment for their spokesmen.

Selbmann tries again to make himself heard. But another
striker jumps onto the table and pushes the Minister aside.
"It's not only a question of norms and prices", he shouts.
"We're not just from the Stalinallee; we're from all over Berlin." And turning to Selbmann: "This is a rising. The Government have made mistakes and must take the consequences. We
demand free Elections and a secret ballot!"

Frantic cheers from the crowd. Another pause. Then a
youngster jumps up to give the men the practical lead they are
waiting for. "Mates, we'll wait half an hour for Ulbricht and
Grotewohl. If they don't give us a hearing, we'll march through
East Berlin. And we'll call a general strike for tomorrow."

Another storm of cheers. Events are taking shape. The first
speaker has named the men's immediate demand: a lowering
of norms and prices. The second has put the fundamental objective: free elections. The third has pointed the way: a general
strike. And the shout echoes round the square: "Down with
the Government! We want free elections!"

The half-hour passes in excited discussion and again the

4. BERLIN, JUNE 17: PEOPLE'S POLICE POST IN FLAMES

5. BERLIN, JUNE 17: AT THE POTZDAMER PLATZ

column forms up. With the men of Block 40 carrying their placard at its head, the procession crosses Unter den Linden and enters the Friedrichstrasse. Chanting in chorus, the men send their slogans ringing through the streets: *"Berliner, reiht euch ein; wir wollen keine Sklaven sein!"* ("Berliners join our ranks; we don't want to be slaves!"). Office workers lean out of their windows to shout encouragement; a woman throws flowers from her balcony. The men are marching eight to ten abreast now and the tail of the procession is half a mile away.

Ahead, in the Wilhelm Pieck Strasse, a police loudspeaker van appears. A voice announces: "The Politbureau of the SED has recommended that the Government reconsider its decree raising the norms. The building workers are requested to disperse and..." A roar of defiance drowns the rest of the sentence—the Politbureau's retreat is several hours too late. The men's original grievance has by now receded into the background; it has served its purpose as a catalyst and the storm, once broken loose, is no longer confined to economic demands. The police loudspeaker van reverses rapidly and disappears from view; the crew of a second, by its inscription the property of the SED, are slower off the mark. So a moment later the demonstrators' own mobile loudspeaker, looking like a carnival float under its load of triumphant pirates, is broadcasting the day's demands from the centre of the procession—calling on the Government to resign, for free all-German elections, for the release of political prisoners, for "butter, not guns", and for a mass meeting at the Strausberger Platz (on the Stalinallee) at 7 o'clock next morning to mark the beginning of a general strike.

The strikers, growing in numbers and confidence with every few hundred yards, march on through hot, dusty streets and back to the Alexanderplatz. Then as the tail of the procession passes the Police Praesidium, a sudden commotion: the loud speaker calls a halt and announces that the police have snatched two men from the crowd and have taken them inside. The strikers, now in an ugly mood, move forward towards the closed doors of the police headquarters. The loudspeaker blares out an ultimatum: if the men are not released within two minutes, the building will be stormed. The People's Police, looking down from their windows, can see that this is not an empty threat: the two men are handed over and the march continues— back to the Stalinallee.

There the procession breaks up. But the news has spread, the astounding story of Berlin's first demonstration against authority in just over two decades, and the streets are full of excited people. The building workers have broken the silence of years; they have torn a web of lies to shreds. This is the moment of truth and of freedom—and some of the onlookers cannot hold back their tears. Nobody looks over his shoulder, or talks in a whisper. And everyone smiles at everyone else.

The centre of the city is simmering and the fever of revolu tion spreads from house to house. It is a fine evening and the Strausberger Platz, where the Stalinallee begins, is black with wildly speculating people. After this, how can the Govern ment possibly stay in power? In the Rosenthaler Platz the crowd is chanting long pent up demands in chorus; at the Oberbaum Bridge men, women and children are happily up rooting the barriers between East and West Berlin. Yet another crowd is milling round the gates of the women's gaol in the

Barnimstrasse, shouting for the release of the political prisoners. Of the People's Police there is no sign.

Using the telephone, the underground, trams and bicycles, scores of self-appointed couriers have carried the call to a general strike to the factories in the suburbs. Half the night-shift at the Bergmann-Borsig engineering works has stayed away. Four hundred men and women of Works I of the nationalised clothing combine "Progress" hurry through the streets to Works II and call out the night-shift there. At the great steelworks in Henningsdorf, on the outskirts of the city, the men hold a meeting and call on SED officials to give an account of themselves. These, protesting their own lack of authority, promise to forward any demands to Party Headquarters in the morning. The steelworkers decide to hold a mass meeting as soon as the day-shift appears.

At Velten, north of the city, the arrival of cyclists from the Stalinallee is the signal for an immediate stoppage of work by the railway construction gangs. The men have been mutinous for weeks: wages and separation allowances for married men have recently been reduced; living quarters in hutted camps are bad; food is scarce; the "Brigadiers" have been ordered to effect a norms increase of no less than 20 per cent; and in reply to complaints, the management has sacked over 200 labourers. The men elect a strike committee and decide to march to Henningsdorf at dawn.

Early that afternoon, three men from the Stalinallee had called at the West Berlin radio station, RIAS, and had given an account of the events leading up to the demonstration. They had also asked to be allowed to broadcast to the Soviet Zone. RIAS is an American institution, however, and it was decided that a broadcast by the strikers themselves would be carrying the station's anti-Communist policy too far. The news of the strike had been carried in the midday bulletin; the news that strikers' representatives were in the radio station was held up until 6.30 p.m. An hour later RIAS announced that the three delegates had drawn up a resolution giving notice that the strike would continue unless the following demands were accepted unreservedly by the government:

1. Payment according to the 'old' norms
2. Immediate measures to reduce the cost of living
3. Free and secret elections
4. No measures to be taken against strikers and their spokesmen.

When the news was over, a familiar voice came on the air. Eberhard Scheutz, RIAS' German programme director, congratulated the East Berlin workers on their victory and pointed out that they had dispelled once and for all the idea that resistance to brutal terror can only take the form of hopeless despair or of martyrdom. He added: "Demand what is reasonable!"

The RIAS news bulletin and Scheutz's commentary penetrated to the furthest corners of the Soviet Zone. At 6 o'clock next morning, the station broadcast a short message from Ernst Scharnowski, trades union leader in West Berlin, calling on members of other trade unions in the Soviet sector not to let the building workers march alone.

It was good advice, but scarcely necessary.

CHAPTER VII

THE RISING

Assembly at the Strausberger Platz ∕ Thirteen miles to Berlin ∕ March on the Government building ∕ Truncheons, stones and armoured cars ∕ Welcome in West Berlin ∕ Fire at Potsdamer Platz ∕ "Lay off the Russians!" ∕ The Lustgarten ∕ Charge of the tanks ∕ The battle of East Berlin ∕ State of emergency ∕ The iron broom ∕ March of the tax collectors ∕ Reprisal ∕ Is the Revolution dead?

JUNE 17, 1953. THE SKY IS DARK AND THREATENING. THE faces of the workers are neither, belying the popular conception of a revolutionary's expression. Hurrying towards the Straus‑ berger Platz by tram, underground and on foot, their morale is soaring—today no one can force them to obey hated orders, or to whisper, keep up pretences and lie. Yesterday gave them victory—and taught them the value of solidarity.

Sixteen miles to the north, the plate‑layers of Velten are marching towards the steelworks at Henningsdorf, collecting reinforcements from factories, workshops and building sites on the way. At Henningsdorf the steelworkers decide at a mass meeting to answer in person the call from the Stalinallee. Man‑ agement and Party officials have kept out of sight; the works police, however, had been told to secure the heavy gates. But the guards are swiftly disarmed; men with crowbars dispose of the locks and 15,000 steelworkers form up in the road out‑ side for a march of 13 miles to the centre of Berlin.

At the Stalin Electric Motor factory in the suburb of Trep‑ tow the 9,000‑strong day‑shift reports for work on time. After half an hour the message flashes through the shops: "Everybody into the yard—strike!" A shop steward proposes a march to the Stalinallee and most of the men start off. A few hundred stay behind and demand to see the managing director, Altenbrandt, who promises them retrospective payment at the old rates and strike pay in addition. Well satisfied, the men hurry off to catch up with the main body.

There were similar scenes in every important factory in East Berlin. Tens of thousands of working-men and women downed tools and made for the Stalinallee to help the building workers complete the job they had begun the day before.

By 7 a.m. the Strausberger Platz was full, with an uncon-cerned, red marble Stalin gazing down at the throng. The building workers formed up to march; thousands fell in behind. In teeming rain and already soaked to the skin, the strikers set off for the House of Ministries in the Leipzigerstrasse.

Few of them appeared to notice two Red Army troop-carriers in a side-street, or a Russian armoured car crossing the Alexanderplatz. Nobody knew that the first mobile battalions of Peoples' Police had set out for Berlin long before midnight, or that Soviet armoured divisions on manoeuvres in the training areas surrounding the capital had been on the move several hours. As on the day before, only occasional fanatics of the FDJ tried to bar the strikers' way. But as the column reached its objective, khaki-clad "barrack-based" police swarmed out of the government building and cordoned off the entrance. Seconds later four, five, seven police trucks swept round a corner, screeched to a halt and spewed forth blue-uniformed civil police, who formed a line across the street. The men at the front of the column tried to halt, but were pushed on by the thousands behind whose view was obstructed. An officer gave the command: "Draw truncheons!", and a hail of blows beat down indiscriminately on the heads and shoulders of the men in front. The strikers tried to defend themselves with fists and feet; they disarmed two policemen and threw two truncheons into a bombed site; but the first casualties fell and half a dozen men were overpowered and dragged away in handcuffs.

The pressure from the vast crowd behind eased at last and the demonstrators disengaged. They took one badly mauled policeman with them. Both sides withdrew until a gap of fifty yards separated them. Then, slowly, the strikers edged forward again to argue with their countrymen in uniform. "Aren't you workers too? Then come over to us!" The crowd spilled over the pavements and on to heaps of rubble between bombed buildings on either side of the street. For several minutes strikers and police stood face to face. Someone threw a stone and, though a few men tried to intervene, others did the same.

At this moment armoured cars appeared—the Red Army had arrived. The armoured cars were followed by steel-helmeted Russian infantry in open trucks. Driving slowly, the Russian vehicles divided the crowd. Some of the strikers moved round to the back of the Government offices and, joining a second column from the Stalinallee, attempted to storm the rear entrance. But this was heavily guarded too.

Spontaneous mass movements are impossible to control and their development is difficult to trace. How many processions were on the streets at this moment, and how strong they were, it was impossible to say. In the operations room at police head-quarters messages from stations and patrol cars overlapped one another; the use of cypher had been abandoned for lack of time to decode and the wall maps had broken out in a bewildering rash of coloured pins.

Shopkeepers lowered their shutters. Offices closed for the day. The suburbs were alive with people converging on the town centre. Trams, underground and overhead railways stop, ped; the transport workers had joined the strike. The Hennings, dorf steelworkers crossed the boundary from the Soviet Zone into the French sector of Berlin: drenched, foot-sore but in high spirits they were taking a short cut through the working-class district of Wedding, once a stronghold of the Communist Party. In the Muellerstrasse their mood infected the West Ber, liners, who poured from shops, offices, homes and pubs to cheer them on. Smiling West Berlin policemen kept the traffic lights at GO; a hastily painted streamer bidding the steel, workers welcome hung from the Council offices; the people of Wedding darted in and out of the briskly moving column, thrusting sandwiches, cigarettes, chocolate, fruit and bottles of beer into grateful hands. For a few minutes the divided city had a chance to show its unity—then, unopposed by a knot of People's Policemen, the men and women from Henningsdorf crossed back into the Soviet sector of the city again. At the big Walter Ulbricht sports stadium they paused to rip the dictator's name from the walls and send his over-life-size portrait up in flames.

By this time the Leipzigerstrasse had been cordoned off and the main body of the strikers was milling round the Potsdamer Platz, where the Russian sector meets the British and American sectors. Red flags, placards, posters, portraits of Russian and German Party leaders, a police hut and boundary posts were blazing.

Mistakenly the demonstrators believed that the House of the

Ministries was the nerve-centre of the regime. No one thought of carrying the assault to the Lothringerstrasse, where the Polit-bureau and the Central Commitee of the SED had their head-quarters. The strikers were without leaders; there was no strategy. Could they have thought that the Russian and Germ-an dictators would give way before a rising of unarmed men? They did believe just this...this was a revolution. But how were the revolutionaries to attain their ends without a general staff to draw up plans of attack, to adapt the tactics of the rising to those of the opponent, to distinguish between possible and im-possible objectives and, above all, to give orders? Soviet tanks were on the way and fists and stones would have to contend with armour plate and machine guns.

Strikers told one another that the West would not let them down; others maintained that the British and Americans could scarcely be expected to put their own tanks against those of the Russians. The West, they argued, must keep out of this: it was a German affair, between people and Government. And when-ever Red Army troops showed themselves, the older men did their best to prevent the crowd from becoming involved with them. "We must show the Russians", they said, "that so far as the working class is concerned, the SED are finished. Then Moscow will have to drop Ulbricht. If we refuse to work for the SED Government, there will have to be new elections." Illusions? Perhaps. And yet the attempt to drive a wedge be-tween the Soviet occupation authorities and the SED leaders showed considerable political sense. If the Russians could be persuaded that their German deputies had lost every shred of authority and respect they would be bound to reconsider their German policy. These were the alternatives: eighteen million restive, sullen German subjects or a united Germany prepared to help in reconciling the conflicting interests of East and West and perhaps willing to take part in a mutually beneficial ex-pansion of trade. Wishful thinking? In the next few days similar arguments were to be put forward by men in the innermost circles of the Party—men who, unless numerous signs deceived, were not without their supporters in the Kremlin itself.

The workers' hopes had firm foundations and their strength, they knew, lay in their numbers. They saw the danger of dis-persion now that their first rallying point at the Government offices was barred to them. The message rippled through the crowd: "To the Lustgarten!"

The Lustgarten, midsummer 1914: Ovation for war; the Kaiser has no use for political parties, only for Germans. Lust-garten, November 1918: Ovation for a sick peace and a tot-tering republic: no one has much use for Germans, only for political parties. Lustgarten 1933: Ovation for future mass-murderers, who have no use for political parties save one. 1950: One Party again—red this time—and the Lustgarten is now called "Marx-Engels Platz".

The Lustgarten was the obvious place at which to re-form. Ten thousand men from Henningsdorf swarmed into the square from the Walter Ulbricht stadium in the Chausseestrasse; another procession had meanwhile formed up in the Stalinallee and moments later twenty thousand men and women—their leaders carrying black, red and gold flags adorned with flowers—marched into the square to the delighted cheers of the earlier arrivals. By midday the Lustgarten was crammed with 50,000 Berliners, straining to hear the hoarse voices of successive speakers from the tribune.

Then, without warning, half a dozen Red Army tanks roared out of a side-street. Moving at full speed into line abreast they charged the crowd. Panic-stricken men and women stampeded in all directions... the Lustgarten was again the Marx-Engels Platz.

Tearing up paving stones as they turned, the tanks pursued a section of the crowd up Unter den Linden. In its wake a tank left the first fatal casualty of the day: the hideously mangled body of a man, caught by the caterpillar tracks, lay in a patch of blood. The strikers made a rough cross out of two pieces of wood and laid it at the spot.

At the top of the street three youngsters, watched by an anxious crowd, had climbed the Brandenburg Gate and were trying to pull down the red flag. Someone shouted: "Come down, they've got a machine-gun trained on you from the Hotel Adlon!" The youngsters, lying flat on their stomachs to present the smallest possible target, hacked at the tough cord with pocket knives. Then, standing recklessly upright, they dropped the flag to the crowd below where it was torn to shreds in an impromptu tug-of-war.

Followed now by armoured cars, the tanks rattled through the Leipzigerstrasse, where the strikers had forced the police cordon round the Government offices to withdraw several yards. A Russian officer, standing in the open turret of his tank, ordered the German police to advance. A hail of stones stopped them short. The tanks moved up; a short burst of machine-gun fire was followed by another... and a third. The strikers rushed for cover among the bombed buildings; casualties were carried into the Western sectors.

The strikers edged forward again. A few linked arms and

advanced on the tanks in line. Some pushed chunks of wood into the tanks' gun barrels; others scrambled on to their turrets and tried to break off the radio aerials. Some dragged lengths of scrap iron from the rubble heaps and tried to jam the tanks' tracks. More bursts of fire; another headlong withdrawal.

Minutes went by while each side waited for the other to make the next move. It was a strange scene; the old heart of Berlin, a maze of burned-out ruins with tufts of grass and rusted iron sprouting from the rubble; thousands of breathless people; clouds of smoke from half a dozen fires; bursts of rifle and machine-gun fire and the roar of tank engines; at the sector boundary, recording vans from the West Berlin radio stations; Press and newsreel photographers with their giant telescopic cameras; ambulances and first aid men. A loudspeaker car, manned by members of a Russian emigré group in West Berlin was begging the Red Army men not to shoot on the workers. Loudspeakers on the eastern side of the square announced: "The Commander of the Red Army garrison in Berlin has proclaimed a state of emergency. The assembly of more than three people is forbidden. Offenders will be punished under martial law."

The demonstrators ignored the warning. At the Alexander-platz another column from the suburbs was stopped by police and troops. But the marchers broke through the cordon and made for the Police Praesidium. Sentries with fixed bay-onets were disarmed; their weapons were smashed against the kerb. Using fire hoses, the police counter-attacked. They were driven back. Four police trucks were overturned and set on fire. Russian infantry arrived, and were received with a salvo of stones. Warnings against provoking the occupation troops were rarer now; desperation had changed the temper of the rising. The young Red Army men observed strict discipline, however. They fired only on direct orders and whenever possible they aimed over the strikers' heads. A few were obviously bewildered; had their comrades not liberated this country in 1945, and were they themselves not here as friends? But most were expressionless: they were not fighting but working. As impersonally as crossing-sweepers, the Russians cleared the Lustgarten, the Leipzigerstrasse, the Alexanderplatz, Unter den Linden.

By mid-afternoon the squares of central Berlin looked like military camps. Groups of men and women wandered, aimlessly now, through the town. Occasional shots rang out still. The plain-clothes men of the State Security Service began their search for scapegoats. Hundreds of strikers made for the safety of the Western sectors; others drifted off home, on foot because public transport was still at a standstill. En route they met more marchers from factories on the outskirts of the city. But it was too late—the rising had been crushed.

The rising was the achievement of the working class: the workers had drawn the rest of the people in their wake. They had succeeded in involving even the "technical intelligentsia"—that select class of men whose services the Communists had secured with high salaries, extra rations and by tolerating their political neutrality. More than 80 per cent of the scientists and technicians employed in the central laboratory at the great electronics factory in Berlin-Koepenick had joined the strikers. Most of the 500 designers and engineers at the Soviet-owned factory "Cable III" had abandoned their work on echo-sounding gear, mine detectors and similar devices and had demonstrated for freedom with the rest. And here and there the strike had affected even the Civil Service.

At the office of the Inspector of Taxes in Berlin-Friedrichs-hain work begins punctually at 7.45 a.m. And so it was on June 17; except that typewriters remained silent and filing cabinets closed. Too excited to work, the Inland Revenue clerks were discussing the events of the previous day. At 9.30 the Branch Secretary of the trade union, Schwarzmüller, called a special meeting of the 256 employees in the canteen and, when all were present, announced with the blandest expression that an extra hour of political instruction had been arranged for the following Saturday. Audible muttering from those at the back swelled to shouts of agreement when someone protested that political schooling was now a thing of the past. Schwarzmüller, manifestly delighted by the reaction to his announcement and certain now of overwhelming support, promptly altered his tone. "Colleagues," he called, "this is our chance to show that the Inland Revenue employees are on the side of the workers! I move that we make a formal declaration of solidarity with the men of the Stalinallee." To loud applause the motion was carried unanimously. And after an unsuccessful attempt by telephone to persuade the staff of head office to go with them, the men and women civil servants marched off in ranks of six abreast to the Stalinallee. "Even the ones with bad feet kept up the pace," one of them related proudly afterwards. They chanted their slogans, called on passers-by to join them and exchanged friendly waves with two People's Policewomen in the back of a passing truck. The march of the Inland Revenue Office ended before the gun muzzles of the Red Army tanks.

German tax collectors striking, demonstrating, rebelling! Men and women who are said to be so steeped in the German conception of duty and absolute obedience to every Govern, ment as to represent Prussian obsequiousness at its most stupid and extreme—this was a revolution indeed!

Meanwhile, in the Potsdamer Platz, the last of the demon, strators were still shouting abuse at the East German soldiery. Shots rang out... slowly the tank turrets revolved, bringing the guns to bear in a silent threat. A wave of bitter, frustrated fury shuddered through the crowd; an eldery man, shouting into the face of a young Russian soldier, yelled for a pistol. "Swine, murderers..."

Strike leaders ran to the British and American authorities, to the West Berlin police and trades union headquarters—begging for support, for weapons. They were everywhere firmly refused.

The end of the revolution? Bitterness, despondency, a sense of utter failure—yes. But not all had lost hope: the strike would go on tomorrow. Curfew at 9 p.m. Red Army troops lit their cooking fires among the ruins; East Berlin had been conquered once again.

Wounded men lay dying in West Berlin hospitals. The Communist radio announced that "the West Berlin provo, cateur", Willi Göttling, had been sentenced to death and shot. Göttling, 36 years old, unemployed and the father of two children, had taken a short cut through the Soviet sector on his way to collect the dole.

Is the revolution dead? What is happening in the Soviet Zone?

CHAPTER VIII

THE "CHAIN REACTION"

I

Brandenburg: outbreak in the rolling-mills ∕ March to the town centre ∕
The judges judged ∕ Tanks ∕ The schoolboys' strike

THIRTEEN CHIMNEYS AND AN EMPTY ADMINISTRATIVE
building: that was all the Soviet dismantling squads left of the
rolling-mills at Brandenburg in 1945. The works had belonged
to the "monopoly-capitalist, profiteer and war-criminal" Flick;
this was reason enough for their nationalisation after the plant
had been removed to Russia. Later it occurred to the Soviet
authorities that the machinery might have been of still greater
value in situ—why deny the Germans the means of production when the product could be removed instead? The new
policy was put into practice and the Soviet-German Government was allowed to create a heavy industry to produce more
iron and steel than ever before. For these were the early years of
the cold war and the Germans, Poles and Czechs were to make
a notable contribution to the Russians' armaments drive.

So the men of Brandenburg rebuilt their rolling-mills—now
their own property, they were told, since they were "the People's"
mills. But the men knew they were working for the Soviet
Union and they were interested in the question of ownership
only insofar as their wages were concerned. If the factory now
belonged to the workers, they argued, then it should pay its
employees a decent wage. And they maintained that the Workers' Government should take steps to see that the workers were

able to buy a respectable piece of sausage for their midday meal. But the shop-stewards' answer was always the same: work harder, they said, or do without.

The compulsory raising of the norms had caused as much bad blood in Brandenburg as it had in the Stalinallee. Everybody felt the necessity for action; no one knew what to do. But when the call came on June 16, all were ready to respond.

As the night shift went to work that evening, a single word was on everyone's lips: Stalinallee... The nightworker's wife had heard it first as she listened to a West Berlin radio station while she prepared her husband's meal. When he woke up she told him the news. Unbelieving, he sat down at the wireless himself—yes, she was right: the Stalinallee builders had marched through East Berlin. On his way to work he met his mates: "In Berlin..." They cut him short; they had already heard. The Berliners had refused to put up with the new norms —there must be action here in Brandenburg too.

At 7 o'clock on the morning of June 17, the Brandenburg building workers downed tools. So did their mates at the new Russian military airfield at Gross-Doelln: two thousand men dropped their picks and shovels, thrashed a trade union official, forced the Party Secretary to hide in the Russian manager's office and looted the H.O. camp shop.

The word "solidarity" had sprung from Berlin to Brandenburg and it assumed the force of law. Men on bicycles sped from building site to factory: "Meet at 7.30 in the yard at the rolling-mills!"

7.30: Two thousand men from inside and outside the rolling-mills gathered in the yard. In a few sentences someone listed the principal demands; another man proposed a demonstration in the town. A third called for a rapid scavenge through the Party offices in the works administrative block; the job was done thoroughly.

A column set off for the town centre, passing two barracks occupied by the Red Army. The sentries watched the marchers curiously but made no attempt to intervene. Reinforced by men from the Thaelmann boat-yard, the strikers halted outside the IFA tractor works, where the factory police, forewarned, had secured the steel gates in order to lock the workers in. A dozen demonstrators ran up with a tree trunk; the gate gave way before the battering-ram and the men from the tractor factory streamed into the road, bringing a number of their heavy vehicles with them.

The strikers made next for the main station to collect the railwaymen. In the square outside, the tractors reduced the SED's propaganda kiosks to matchwood. On to the district headquarters of the SED, where six policemen were guarding the entrance with drawn pistols. The strikers kept their distance. But some of the younger men climbed the face of the building, scrambled through an open window and, rushing down the stairs, took the police from the rear. Their weapons were thrown into the river; files, Party literature and portraits of the leaders were piled in the street. Another crowd stormed the Party's area headquarters nearby. Here the police showed no inclination to die a hero's death for the State: they surrendered their rifles hastily and the office was cleared of documents and propaganda material in a few minutes.

The strikers' next objective, the headquarters of the trades union movement, was an historic building. In 1850 it had been the seat of a court set up to try the local leaders of the 1848 revolution; and the scene of repeated demonstrations for their release. 1848 and 1953—would the revolution against the tyrants of the twentieth century succeed?

11 a.m. The workers were no longer alone; their marching columns had sucked the people from their homes and all Brandenburg was on the streets. Their great objective was freedom, but there was an immediate, more tangible target too.

When, a few days before, the Politbureau had announced the "new course", the Brandenburgers' first thought had been for the political prisoners. On June 12 they had taken part in a demonstration which was neither arranged by the Party nor obstructed by the police. The employees of a haulage contractor named Taege had gone in a body to the local gaol to ask for the release of their boss, who was serving a three years' sentence for "economic crimes". It was a peaceable occasion—some of the men were carrying flowers—and Taege, after some discussion between the crowd and the prison authorities, was indeed released.

Today the demonstrators made for the combined prison and magistrates court in the Steinstrasse, where they waited quietly for the police guard to admit a delegation. But the police slammed the shutters. Impatiently, the strikers surged forward; the police fired their weapons, aiming high. But some of the men had acquired weapons of their own and a carpenter, crouching behind a pillar, delivered an ultimatum. Together with four others, he was admitted—and the police soon surrendered.

The five strikers, accompanied by a magistrate and a number of warders, went through the gaol calling the political prisoners from their cells. One man could not be moved; they found him, bandaged about the head and apparently out of his senses, on the floor of his cell. The remainder—thirty men and women scarcely able to grasp what had happened—were brought into the street, to be carried away on the shoulders of a frenziedly cheering crowd.

At this moment a well-known face appeared at a window: it was Benkendorf, a "People's Judge" notorious for his sentences of three years' imprisonment for such petty thefts as a handful of nails (unobtainable by lawful means) from a nationalised factory. The crowd shouted to him to come down and account for himself. But the judge hid and, discovered at length by the carpenter, begged to be locked in a cell. The carpenter agreed, and did his best to persuade the crowd that it was better so. But someone shouted that Benkendorf should be tried in the market square and the proposal met with a roar of approval. So Benkendorf—together with the Public Prosecutor, Bechtel, who was found in his office—was brought out in handcuffs.

Judge and Prosecutor were marched off at the head of a great procession to the market square. Some of the demonstrators were in an ugly mood, however, and both men were badly beaten up on the way. Finally they were carried on to the tribune erected for the use of visiting political dignitaries on ceremonial occasions and five thousand people attempted to interrogate them. Neither man was in a condition to reply. The Prosecutor was unconscious and Judge Benkendorf could barely stammer that he was "in duty bound to act according to instructions received from superiors". Howls of rage from those within earshot: "Hang them both!" Strike leaders restored order with difficulty; Benkendorf and Bechtel were taken away in an ambulance. However, it was too late: both were to die of their injuries in hospital.

About the same hour demonstrators were marching through the little town of Rathenow, building workers and employees of the optical instruments factory leading the way. As they passed an H.O. shop, someone caught sight of a man who was widely known as a stool-pigeon in the pay of the security police: his name was Hagedorn. The man backed into the shop. But the strikers stopped and called him out into the street. As he obeyed, a small boy called out: "That's the man who sent my father to prison!" Eye-witnesses later claimed to have seen Hagedorn aim a blow at the boy with a cosh—whether this was true or not, the temper of the crowd suddenly changed: Hagedorn was swept into the middle of the mob, punched and beaten, dragged to the river bank and hurled into the water. Barely keeping afloat, he swam to the opposite bank—but men and women were there to push him back. Bleeding and exhausted, their victim beat at the muddy water, to be rescued at last by the police. Before he could be brought to an ambulance the crowd were at him again, demanding to know how many people he had denounced to the Communist Gestapo. But Hagedorn was unconscious. A few hours later he died.

At midday a factory worker burst into a classroom at the Brandenburg Technical College. "The People's Police are firing on German working-men!" he shouted. The students rushed for the door and joined a crowd hurrying to the central police station. Intent on freeing more political prisoners, the strikers had stormed the building and had cut fire hoses used by the police in its defence. Barrack-based police arrived in trucks; two were overturned. The strikers broke into the prison yard. The police opened fire and three men dropped to the ground, wounded. The rest ran for cover and prepared for a second assault. Then Soviet troops appeared—six lorry-loads of heavily armed infantry.

Two hours before, the police had been surrendering their weapons. Now—reinforced by the Red Army—they were shooting. Earlier, as the demonstrators marched past their barracks, the Russians had kept out of sight; now their tanks were grinding through the streets while infantrymen patrolled the pavements.

At 5 p.m. the Soviet Commandant declared a state of emergency and Russian troops, well disciplined but firm, began to clear the streets. The State Security Service came out in force—rounding up hundreds of strikers and crowding them into the gaols they had opened up only a few hours before.

Tired and dispirited, the strikers drifted back to their homes. Those who lived in the country returned to their villages and told their astonished neighbours of the events of the day. They spoke of their defeat, of the dead, wounded and arrested. But they also described the brief but glorious hours of victory: telling of the freeing of the prisoners, of the assault on the Party buildings, of justice in the market place.

The bigger factories—in spite of Soviet tanks on the premises—continued the strike until June 19 in an attempt to secure the release of their arrested colleagues. By and large the men were successful and on June 20 the last strikers went back to work—at go-slow pace. Perhaps the last to demonstrate were the secondary schoolboys in the Heinrich-von-Kleist Strasse, the overwhelming majority of whom were members of the Communist youth organisation. At a demonstration on July 3 to call attention to their demand for the deletion from their time-tables of political instruction and Russian grammar, the boys forced their teachers to lock themselves in a common room and the headmaster to telephone for assistance. While six truck-loads of police surrounded the school an officer went from class to class appealing to reason: "Your parents, after all, returned to work several days ago..."

2

Inter-zonal train Berlin-Magdeburg • "Set the political prisoners free!"
The rising crushed • The smaller towns follow suit • Legality in Thale

Berlin railway stations... it has been said that their worth today lies in their scrap and in their considerable sentimental value. The Anhalter, Lehrter, Stettiner and Potsdamer Stations are dead and all but forgotten. From the Schlesischer Station an occasional train departs for Warsaw and Moscow; the Frie-drichstrasse Station sends passengers on their weary way to Saxony and Thuringia; the expresses that pass through the Zoo Station in the space of twenty-four hours can be counted on the fingers of two hands. The strands that bound Berlin with the West and with the provincial towns of Central Ger-many have worn thin.

On June 17 the crowded inter-zonal train to Hanover left the Zoo Station in West Berlin at 8.52 a.m. as usual. But today nobody talked about the weather, railway delays or minor ill-nesses; the passengers were all discussing the news of the previous afternoon from the other half of the city.

Shortly before midday the train steamed into Magdeburg. One of the passengers reported later: "As we drew into the station we were startled by a tremendous din. The platform, normally deserted while the inter-zonal train passes through, was black with wildly cheering men and women. Boarding the train they swept through the corridors and into the compartments, laughing and throwing their arms round our necks. Outside, people were shouting: 'It's all over! We're free! The SED will have to resign!' We handed round cigarettes and fruit, but above all they wanted Western newspapers. 'What's happening in Berlin this morning?' they asked. 'Are they on strike too? We're from the Thaelmann heavy engineering works—we were the first to strike. Now the whole of Magdeburg has come out. Where are you from? Bonn! Don't forget us. Don't let us down!'

"Red flags and placards were being trampled in the dirt and there was not a policeman in sight. Two youngsters chalked slogans on the sides of the carriages: 'Greetings from free Magdeburg' and 'Free elections in all Germany'. Twenty minutes later our train pulled out of the station and from the windows we could see great crowds in the streets. On the outskirts of the town a seemingly endless column was tramping along a parallel railway track, presumably making for a prison which lies further up the line."

In Magdeburg half a dozen heavy engineering works—both Soviet and "People's" property—had formed the backbone of a strike which began in the Thaelmann works at 7.30 a.m. and spread within two hours to the power station, gas works, tram service, main post office, local government and virtually every other factory in the town. The demonstrators' first objectives were the "House of German-Soviet Friendship", the district offices of the SED, the Free German Youth headquarters and the editorial offices of the local SED newspaper—all these were thoroughly cleared of propaganda literature and portraits of the Communist leaders.

At midday the bulk of the strikers massed in front of the Police Praesidium, while motor-cyclists dashed through the streets to round up stragglers. The crowd pressed forward, shouting for the release of the political prisoners inside; a Red Army patrol vanished round a corner. German police officers guarding the main gate, realising that their position was hopeless, asked for five minutes' grace—and then for another five minutes. But the crowd was rapidly losing patience. Pushing the police out of the way, the strikers went for the gate with crow-bars. Shots rang out; two men dropped to the ground; someone was firing from a roof. Then more shots... this time a policeman went down. A handful of strikers had occupied the court-house next door and were firing from the windows with captured police rifles. Down below, the men grabbed an armed policewoman whom they suspected of having opened fire. She was stripped to the skin and badly beaten up. Then two police inspectors shouted to the crowd that the political prisoners would be released as soon as they could be separated from the criminal cases. But the files could not be found and some thirty prisoners—criminal and political cases together—were set free.

In the suburb of Sudenburg an attempt to storm the prison failed completely: the strikers ran into the concentrated fire of the People's Police and several men were killed and wounded. Three weeks later a market gardener, Ernst Jennrich, was sentenced to death for taking part in an armed attack on the Sudenburg prison in which three policemen had lost their lives.

At the gaol for prisoners under interrogation in Magdeburg-Neustadt, the morning begins like any other. About 10 o'clock the men and women in the cells hear warders running through the corridors and shouting that all windows are to be closed immediately. The usual half-hour of exercise in the yard is cancelled. At midday there are more agitated footsteps in the corridors. Faint cries can be heard: "Freedom..." The prisoners look at one another, decide that someone in solitary confine-ment has had a breakdown. But the shouts are louder now: "Freedom... freedom... we're coming to fetch you out..." The noise is coming from outside. Warders rush up the stairs and the prisoners, drumming with their fists and heels against the doors of their cells, join in the shouting: "Freedom... let us out!" Outside, a crash and the sound of splintering wood, followed by the noise of hundreds of feet rushing across the courtyard. Cell doors are burst open; three hundred men and women run into the yard, whooping, laughing, crying. Some are very quiet. A few warders come out of their hiding-place under the roof and agree to distribute identity cards and the prisoners' own clothes. A Russian armoured car has taken up position at the prison gate, but the crew make no attempt to intervene. Free again, the prisoners are in no hurry: the strikers rule the streets, the police are cowering, the Russians are minding their own business... the revolution has succeeded and everything has changed. Why worry?

Within a few hours, most of the prisoners were re-arrested. The man who was responsible for this account washed and shaved at a friend's house in the town, changed his clothes, borrowed some money and walked to the station. There were no trains. He walked on to the station at Neustadt, took a suburban train and reached Potsdam after three or four changes. Several days later he managed to slip across the border into West Berlin.

Towards 1 p.m. two Red Army tanks and a troop of armoured cars appeared in the centre of Magdeburg leading 25–30 troop-carrying trucks, some of them towing anti-aircraft and anti-tank guns. Firing warning shots into the air, the Russians cleared a way through the crowd. A Red Army officer asked the nearest striker what all the trouble was about, and was told in no uncertain terms. A tank turret opened and the SED District Secretary, Sepp Fischer, emerged. Unwisely, he tried to address the crowd... "Fetch him down! String him up!" Fischer ducked—but he was not quick enough; badly cut about the head by flying stones, he had to be carried off by Russian soldiers.

The Soviet Commandant declared a state of emergency; Russian troops occupied the factories and the prisons filled again. A Soviet military court sentenced two workers to be shot. Fear and misery crept through the town.

In the big factories the strike continued next day. At the Thaelmann works, the men tried to stage a mass meeting in protest against the arrest of twenty of their mates—it was broken up by Russian troops. At the Karl Liebknecht heavy engineering works in Buckau some fifty men were arrested by Russian soldiers and German police. There were reports of more than 700 arrests in all.

Work was resumed on the nineteenth. That morning the employees of the ship-building yard at Rothensee announced their intention to elect new trade union representatives: Russian tanks broke up the meeting. On the twentieth, two hundred and eighty employees of one of the smaller factories in Branden-burg signed a resolution demanding the Government's resig-nation. On June 27 the pattern shed at the Dimitrov works was destroyed by fire.

Russian security officers installed themselves in the prisons. Interrogating—as is their custom—by night, they neither struck nor shouted at the men before them. Quietly, almost politely, they asked about the "organisers" of the rising, about the course of events, the strikers' objectives and intentions, and inquired into the reasons for their hatred of the regime. But before their turn came to be interrogated the arrested men were made to stand for long periods in the prison yard, facing a wall chipped with bullet marks. In a crowded room in the Police Praesidium fifty or sixty prisoners sat close together on narrow benches, twisted with pain. They were forbidden to speak, stand up or move. There they sat for two days, three days, in some cases four and five days on end. Three times a day they were given a slice of dry bread and a mug of cold coffee. Once a day they were taken to the lavatories.

In Magdeburg and the neighbouring towns of Calbe and Stass-furt the demonstrations began and ended on Wednesday, June 17. The wave of unrest reached the smaller towns close to the zonal border a day later: here it was largely the news of the the brutal suppression of the strikes in the big industrial centres which drove the people into open resistance.

At Wernigerode, on June 18, engineering workers set out for the neighbouring town of Ilsenburg on the zonal border, where they hoped to uproot the frontier posts and march in triumph into the Federal Republic. But they ran into road-blocks manned by the Red Army and were forced to withdraw under fire. The unrest in this border district continued for several days.

In Halberstadt, Wednesday and Thursday were uneventful working days; on Friday, June 19, employees of the smaller factories resolved to strike, elected spokesmen and demanded a reduction of norms and of prices, the Government's resignation and free elections. They also called for the immediate punishment of those who had ordered the People's Police to fire on the strikers in Magdeburg and Berlin. Later that morning, as the workers streamed into the streets, a voice announced over the town's loud-speaker system that a state of emergency had been declared—a manoeuvre which almost persuaded the strike committees to call off the proposed demonstration. Excitement however, was already too great and by midday five thousand people, mostly young men and girls, stood shoulder to shoulder in the market square. But the Red Army had arrived in the town on the previous evening, and half an hour later a company of infantry, escorted by a tank and two light anti-aircraft guns, took up positions. Firing warning shots into the air, the Russians scattered the crowd, arresting about one hundred men women and children—almost all were released in the next few days. From 3 p.m. until late that evening a central strike committee negotiated with members of the town council, agreeing finally to return to work next day in exchange for a promise that their demands would be forwarded to Berlin through official channels. At 10 p.m. police loudspeaker vans toured the streets announcing the terms of the agreement.

It is worth recording that every factory in this typically quiet medium-sized German town took part in the strike: the 1,300 employees of the railway repair works, the 900 men of the EKM-diesel engine factory, the 1,200 building workers, the 120 employees of three nationalised automobile workshops, the 200 women and girls at the H.O. State Trading Organisation, the 25 members of the Central Planning Office, and, finally, the employees of the town's last three privately-owned factories. The only exception was the nationalised bacon and sausage factory, where production continued by permission of all the strike committees.

The German's habitual concern for order and legality was particularly noticeable in the smaller towns and it often confused the adversary. At the steelworks at Thale, for example, each department elected its own strike committee and sent its representatives to deliver formal strike notices to the local trade union headquarters, whose officials had no alternative but to recognise the strike as legal. A demonstration followed: after the town had been cleared of superfluous paper and bunting, four thousand factory workers assembled in the yard at the steelworks, and the Communist mayor attempted to make a speech. But he was shouted down, forced to remove his Party badge and was bundled off home. The works manager suffered a similar indignity. Later, the meeting was broken up by Soviet troops—and during the night all members of strike committees were arrested. Next day, with the factory surrounded by a cordon of tanks, Russian officers threatened that all the "ringleaders" would be shot if work was not resumed. The men gave in a day later, on June 19. But hundreds of them handed in their union cards and cancelled their membership of the Society for German-Soviet Friendship, maintaining that the Russians' attitude was incompatible with the supposed ideals of the latter organisation. On July 4 they staged a sit-down strike and secured the release of a number of the strike leaders.

Couriers from Thale had spread the strike to Quedlinburg, where 7,000 people, massed in the main square to demonstrate for the Government's resignation, cheered themselves hoarse when a war widow dashed into the Town Hall and hauled down the red flag. The mayor, who tried to intervene, was beaten up; so was the director of the H.O. trading organisation. Meanwhile, other strikers had besieged the local headquarters of the SED, where the Comrades had locked themselves in. A tractor from a local State farm smashed the stout, iron-bound doors and the First Secretary of the SED district organisation was rewarded for his loyalty to the Party with a sound thrashing. He was finally liberated by 30 Russian soldiers. At 6 p.m. Soviet armoured cars moved in; a state of emergency was declared. Machine-guns were posted at intervals of a few hundred yards in the main streets and at the railway station, while anti-tank guns guarded the town exits. In spite of the imposition of a curfew, small groups of people remained in the streets all night, and at 5 o'clock next morning a party of young strikers broke into the Technical College and ransacked the Party library. At noon on June 18 a column of farmers arrived from Wetterstedt intending to reinforce the factory workers— Russian troops stopped them at the outskirts of the town, however. That afternoon the employees of the Mewe metal-ware factory sent a four-man delegation to inform the Soviet Town Commandant that the strike was directed not against the occupation force but exclusively against the East German Government. One man was received; he did not return. On the nineteenth the security police arrested 40 employees of the metal-ware factory and 70 townspeople, among them the woman who had hauled down the red flag. The strike ended on June 22.

3

The "red heart of the Reich" ⁄ The Leuna story ⁄ Solidarity with Berlin ⁄ March to Merseburg ⁄ Halle ⁄ Casualties at the Kirchtor prison ⁄ Mass meeting in the market square ⁄ Central strike committee ⁄ The beginnings of organisation ⁄ Free for a day ⁄ Water cell at Bitter⁄ feld ⁄ Strike at the Mansfeld copper combine ⁄ Leipzig: the East German façade

Germany's chemical-producing area is a land of chimneys, acrid smoke, grey factories and regular rows of dreary little houses. Born of two great wars, the "Red heart of the Reich" has played a leading rôle in the story of German revolutionary movements—the Leuna chemical works was built in 1916; its sister concern, Buna, owes its existence to the re-armament drive of Hitler's Third Reich. Tens of thousands of labourers, uprooted from their homes, built the great factories and turned carbon, oils and acids into synthetic products for war. Separ-ated from their families, they lived in overcrowded camps in a world of labour unrelieved by material comforts or mental distraction: it was an artificial climate well suited to the propa-gation of the seeds of revolution.

At the Leuna works, notices warning against explosions might well have applied as much to the workers as to the inflammable liquid fuel they produced. In November 1918 Leuna had greeted the news of the naval mutiny at Kiel by hoisting the red flag. Tens of thousands of Leuna men had marched to Merseburg, bringing the miners and other workers out on strike with them. They came out in March 1919. They did so again in 1920, when the right-wing Kapp battalions attempted their *coup d'état*. The Leuna workers stood "on the Left, where the heart is"; in March 1921, when the Communists struck what was to be the decisive blow against the young German democracy, they revolted again. A Communist historian wrote of them thirty years later: "On March 21, 1921, the battle began in the area of Hettstedt, Eisleben, Erfurt, and west of the Bitterfeld-Halle-Merseburg railway line. The counter-revolutionaries were served by 39 companies of police and a Reichswehr howitzer battery. Throughout the grim battle against the soldiery, the revolutionary working class fought like heroes. Around Mansfeld and at Leuna the battle raged for days and the Leuna bosses fled for their lives. After the great factory had been surrounded, the police moved in to the assault... Four weeks later the Police Commandant reported that he had been able to suppress the rising."*

The story of the Leuna works—was history to repeat itself? Early on June 17 three thousand men and women ran into the yard outside Block 24 and resolved to strike. The spark from Berlin! Over the years the fuze had grown... U.S. bombers had dropped thousands of tons of steel and high explosive, had sown destruction and horror, had reduced a mighty industry to ruins. What remained was taken from the I. G. Farben concern by the Russian victors. The workers set about the task of rebuilding. But the fruits of their labours belonged to a Soviet Corporation and bore the name of a

* From an article by Bernhard Koenen in the factory newspaper *Leuna Echo* of 28.3.51.

man who had risen from the ranks of the revolutionaries to the position of dictator: Leuna became the Walter Ulbricht Works.

More than twenty thousand men and women worked in day- and night-shifts; a small army of scientists, chemists and engineers calculated, experimented, constructed—for Soviet Russia. The working-men and women were left with high prices, inadequate wages and back-breaking norms; when the price of meat went up, or when the worker's railway ticket was abolished, they were not consulted. The old unrest began to show. Indeed, it had never quite died down. In 1951, when the Government decided that the workers themselves should accept the system of exploitation embodied in the collective wages contracts, Leuna had offered open resistance. The men had mutinied, and secured concessions. The 28,000 were strong and not to be gagged. And when the new norms were intro-duced they did not trouble to hide their disgust.

A week earlier the security police had made fifteen arrests. Today men on bicycles dashed from building to building: "Mass meeting outside the administrative block!" Ten thous-and answered the call, soon they were fifteen thousand, finally twenty thousand. Party officials—the SED had its district head-quarters on the premises—did their best to take over the plat-form, inviting the men to appoint representatives to negotiate about the norms. But negotiation had been forbidden and now it was too late. Somebody shouted from the crowd: "We're here to show our solidarity with Berlin!" The SED First Secretary was elbowed aside, and successive speakers put forward an imposing list of demands: wages, prices, norms, disarming of the works police, replacement of union officials, dismissal of

SED officials, renaming of the factory—a board with Ulbricht's name was ripped from the wall and smashed. They also called for the Government's resignation and for free elections; for the unconditional release of all political prisoners. They elected spokesmen and sent them to the management: the Russians were courteous, but made no promises.

Returning to the yard the delegates enjoined the strikers to refrain from damaging works property and above all from provoking the Russians. They also announced that Buna and other factories were on strike, that the town of Halle was in a state of insurrection, that the Buna workers were marching on Merseburg.

The meeting broke up. A few thousand returned to work to maintain production; the remainder set off to join up with the men from Buna. A few minutes later two butchers, on their way home from Merseburg with a van-load of meat, were waved to a stop by men on motor-cycles. "Leuna are marching —get off the road!"

And there they were, a broad and seemingly endless column, singing the revolutionary songs of their fathers and shouting in chorus for the Government's resignation. In the villages, doors and windows opened and women waved them on. The two butchers hurried on to Rossbach, where they made straight for the lignite works and reported what they had seen and heard. The strike spread.

Leuna and Buna men met in Merseburg at midday. It was a triumphal entry. Directed from loudspeaker vans by their strike leaders, they ransacked Party offices, stormed the police station and broke into the prison, where they destroyed the files and released the political prisoners.

There was no one to resist them and there seemed nothing more to do. Most of the men returned to the factories; some set off for Halle.

In Halle the strike was complete. Led by 8,000 men from the railway works at nearby Ammendorf, three separate processions had swept through the town, leaving a trail of red flags, posters and placards behind them. The Council offices and the district and area headquarters of the SED were all in the hands of the strikers. An attack on the prison in the Steinstrasse was no less successful. As the crowd approached the gates, police on the roof opened fire. Nobody was hit, however, and all the prisoners—most of them women—were released from their cells and handed over to friends and relations outside. At the courthouse next door the strikers found a police inspector; suspecting that he had given the order to fire, they beat him up. A policewoman caught fumbling with a pistol was handled no less roughly. On to the main prison at the Kirchtor. Here the gates were locked, barred and barricaded from within, and police guards crouched at the windows with automatic rifles. Outside, the vast crowd milled to and fro... suddenly the gate gave way and the crowd swept into the yard. A burst of fire—several men dropped. Another burst—the crowd fell back, dragging the seriously wounded to shelter. They did not attack again.

Russian troops had been patrolling the town since the middle of the morning. But they had made no attempt to intervene, ignoring the marchers, the cheers and the jeers. An officer, bespattered by a young hothead, quietly brushed the mud off his tunic.

At about 1 p.m. between 30,000 and 40,000 people swarmed into the lower of Halle's two market squares while a handful of

Befehl!

Ueber die Stadt Halle ist der

A u s n a h m e z u s t a n d

verhangt. Demonstrationen,
Versammlungen und Zusam-
menrottungen jeder Art sind
verboten.

Jeder Aufenthalt auf den
Straßen ist von

21.00 bis 4 Uhr

verboten.

Im Falle von Widerstand
wird von der Waffe Gebrauch
gemacht!

Halle, den 17. Juni 1953

Chef der Garnison und Militär-
kommandant der Stadt Halle
(Saale)

HALLE: PROCLAMATION OF STATE OF EMERGENCY

determined men stood to one side and discussed the next move. The factories, streets and administrative centres had been taken over—except for the central post office, which the police had secured early that morning—and the attack must not be allowed to peter out. The Government appeared to have capitulated and someone, they decided, must take over power and responsibility for affairs. The men introduced themselves to the crowd and were accepted as members of a central strike committee: a businessman, an employee of the H.O. trading organisation, a medical student, a Leuna-worker, a Buna-worker and an employee of the Halle Engineering Works. The committee's first decision was approved by a show of hands; the local radio transmitter and a printing press must be requisitioned. Another mass meeting was arranged for 6 p.m.

The plan to take over the transmitter had to be abandoned; it had been out of order for several weeks. Four members of the committee called at the editorial office of the local Christian Democratic Party newspaper, and the management, after consultation with SED and union officials, agreed to publish a leaflet. But somebody telephoned the security police, and the strike leaders were compelled to beat a hasty retreat.

At 6 o'clock the market square was crowded as never before. At least 60,000 people had turned out to celebrate their first free day for over twenty years. The businessman stepped to the microphone. He spoke of East Berlin's example on the previous day and, interrupted by wild applause at every second sentence, he enumerated the people's charges against the Government. He called for a general strike to enforce elections and for the release of all political prisoners. And he asked the crowd to observe strict discipline, warning against panic buying, looting and violence—the Red Army, he told them earnestly, must be given no excuse to intervene.

The H.O. employee, acting as chairman of the meeting, put the principal points of the committee's programme to a vote: they were carried by acclamation. Five other speakers took their turn at the microphone...

Then, crawling down the slope from the upper market, Red Army tanks entered the square. Laughter died away. Yard by yard, singing the National Anthem as they retreated, the people gave way. Halle had been free for a day. Leaflets, fluttering down from the upper market, proclaimed a state of emergency. Soon the streets were full of Russian and German infantry.

A bitter evening; a dozen people had died in the streets that day, more died of wounds in hospital. The security police came out of hiding and combed the town for victims.

The Central Strike Committee, intending to call another mass rally and to take over the city administration, had arranged to meet again at 7 o'clock next morning. But only two of the eight men appeared at the appointed time; the others had either been arrested or had fled. Sadly the last two strike leaders set out for West Berlin.

At Leuna, most of the strikers had returned to the works by mid-afternoon on the day of the rising. It was reported that the Soviet managing director had received the men's representatives and that he appeared willing to grant their demands so far as lay in his power. A member of the strike committee seemed satisfied with this result and recommended a return to work. At that moment another strike leader announced over the internal loud-speaker system that four men had been arrested;

the strike, he said, must continue until all four had been re-leased. The men, waiting for news outside the administrative building, agreed. At four o'clock Russian tanks drove through the gates. The strike leaders demanded that the tanks be with-drawn; the strike, they said, would otherwise continue. For a time there was deadlock. Then a Russian colonel agreed to withdraw the tanks if the men's leaders would guarantee to keep order. But it was too late. Rioting broke out in the yard and the tanks stayed. They remained at Leuna for several days.

At Buna, work was resumed on the same afternoon. But the factory was nevertheless occupied by the Red Army, and 134 employees, including all members of the strike committee, save one, were arrested. So the strike began again. It continued until June 20 when, after three meetings between the strikers' single remaining representative and the senior Russian director, 130 of those arrested had been released and the Red Army units (an infantry battalion, a squadron of reconnaissance troops, 14 tanks, 14 anti-aircraft guns) were withdrawn from the factory area.

On the morning of the seventeenth some 15,000 men and women from the dyestuffs and film factories at Wolfen marched to Bitterfeld, where they joined another 10,000 men from the big "Electrochemical Combine" and the employees of half-a-dozen lesser concerns. By the middle of the morning the rail-waymen and power-station workers had joined them; at noon a crowd of over 50,000 collected in the "Square of Youth" to approve a strike committee consisting of a local teacher, a re-presentative of each of the larger factories, a university student and a housewife. The teacher called out a list of objectives to be occupied: the central police station, the court-house, the prison, the town hall and all buildings belonging to the Party. The crowd split up. The biggest group made for the combined court-house and gaol—and arrived simultaneously with two truck-loads of blue uniformed People's Police. The luckless guardians of the law, dragged from their vehicles and roughly disarmed, presented no problem. Nor did the prison gates. An official in the public prosecutor's office was made to produce a list of the political prisoners, the police superintendent was persuaded to sign discharge certificates. Meanwhile all the cells had been opened and the criminal cases had disappeared with the rest, though a bicycle thief and a man serving a sentence for indecent assault were recognised and recovered. The warders, who seemed likely to be lynched, were locked in the cellar —but not before their chief, Geiser, had been paid in kind for past brutalities. Two men who were known to have worked for the security police were also taken into protective custody.

Near the station passers-by were being invited by strikers to view the security police headquarters, a large white building which had been found empty. The prisoners had been trans-ported elsewhere and only one official had stayed behind. Dis-covered in a cupboard, he was half beaten to death. In the basement strikers found the notorious water-torture cells: tiled boxes three and a half feet high and four feet wide in which the victim, who was unable to stand upright, was half immersed in cold water.

After the prisoners had been freed, the strikers dispersed. An hour later the Red Army moved in. Infantry cleared the streets and re-occupied public buildings while armoured units went into the factories.

More than thirty years earlier the strikers' fathers—and indeed some of the older men among them—had marched beneath the red flag which they were trampling in the dirt this day. As the shock troops of the left-wing rising of the 'twenties, they had marched and fought in Leuna and in Halle, and in the mining area around Hettstedt and Eisleben. In those days Wilhelm Pieck was a young, largely unknown Comrade; now the Mansfeld Copper Combine bore his name. The miners had made no objection. But on June 17 they shouted that the "People's President" must go. They marched to Eisleben, where they found some 1,500 people—housewives, building-workers and youths of the FDJ in their blue shirts—already demonstrating in the market square. They pushed on to the central police station in the Freistrasse. Four Russian sentries decamped hurriedly; twenty-five People's Policemen willingly gave up their weapons. The miners removed the files and marched to the gaol, beside the law courts. Five police guards gazed anxiously at the advancing column, then plucked up their courage and slammed shut the heavy gate. It was broken down with crow-bars. The police made no further attempt to resist; but the warder refused to hand over the keys. The cells were broken into and more than a hundred prisoners were handed their identity cards and released. Finally, the miners ransacked the Public Prosecutor's office.

Later they returned to the pits and stormed the main admin-istrative block, paying particular attention to the norms de-partment and destroying all records of the output of individual "brigades". That evening the men from the "Otto-Brosowsky" pit released about one hundred political prisoners who had been put to forced labour under appalling conditions underground. Early on the eighteenth, the men of the "August Bebel" copper foundry elected a strike committee. The works manager thundered about "provocateurs from Berlin"; they smashed a picture of Ulbricht over his head. Then the miners marched to Helbra. The entire Mansfeld Combine (with the exception of the Karl Liebknecht foundry) was in a state of insurrection. The strike continued until June 20.

Just to the north, at Hettstedt, about 5,000 employees of the rolling mills joined the strike in the late afternoon of the seventeenth, when they heard that Soviet troops were in action against the strikers in Berlin. The Russian managing director tried to calm the men down, promising that their wage demands would be met. But no one would listen, and the men set off for the town where they wandered about aimlessly, without leaders to draw up a plan of campaign. At 8 p.m. a state of emergency was declared; later still the rolling mills were occupied by Red Army units. Next day the men arrived at work to find tanks at the main gate. Most of them promptly went home again and did not return to work until June 22.

It has been said that the people of Leipzig are more fortunate than their compatriots in other parts in the Soviet Zone, in that their city's rôle as a shop window for "Socialism" has brought them some relief from the cruder, outward signs of Communist rule. Certainly the regime, with an eye to the susceptibilities of the Western visitor to Leipzig's biennial trade fair, has avoided imposing the Communist imprint too strongly and allowed the city to preserve some of its more harmless "bour-geois" characteristics. It has been a sound policy: many Western businessmen have returned from their excursion be-

hind the Iron Curtain to report (as they did of Nazi Germany
in earlier years) that "it's not really so bad over there", that
there are goods in the shops, that the German Communists
seem to be "perfectly reasonable people". The citizens of Leipzig live behind the façade, however. For years, as the opening
day of the fair approaches, they have watched prices fall a
little, shop windows fill and H.O. restaurant menus lengthen
a little. But after the fair the city has quickly returned to
normality; for ten months of the year, life in Leipzig is like life
in any other East German provincial town.

On June 17, however, the people were in carnival mood.
The law of solidarity had emptied the factories and by noon
half the town was on the streets. Laughing and cheering, they
surged through the city, ransacking Party offices, and filling the
gutters with political tracts and portraits of the Communist
hierarchy.

Later the police recovered their nerve, firing into the thick
of a crowd assaulting the main prison. Despite the casualties—
some of them fatal—the strikers attacked a second time; and
again the police opened fire. A third attack... another burst of
fire... more casualties.

The revolution had taken its toll of men's lives. The assault
had been beaten back, the demonstrators scattered. Yet they
rallied again. Eye-witnesses reported later: "In complete silence
a procession filed slowly through the Petersstrasse, at its head
men carried the first fatal casualty of the day on a stretcher, a
young man shot in the head. A wreath lay across his body, and
people threw flowers as the cortège drew past. The surrounding
streets were deserted, and there was hate and bitterness in the
air."

And the eye-witnesses added that the second attack would have been grimmer and more determined still. But Red Army tanks had reached the town hall square and Russian and German infantrymen soon followed. Gradually—the Russians firing high in the air, the Germans into the crowd—the soldiers drove the strikers off the streets and into their homes, where they waited, dejected and afraid for their families and themselves, for the morrow. But the strikers had discovered their strength: tomorrow, they said, we go on... Next morning the men found their factories guarded by tanks and occupied by troops. They refused to work. They squatted in front of their lathes and benches and turned their backs on Party officials. They tore up their union cards and demanded that their arrested mates be freed. And when the pressure on them became unbearable, they worked at a snail's pace. It was announced that three young men—aged 17, 24 and 25—had been executed by order of the Soviet Military Commandant. It was estimated that 30 people had lost their lives, that more than 100 were wounded in the streets. A casualty list for Leipzig—or any other centre of the rising—has not been published to this day.

Leipzig remained in a state of siege for several weeks and trouble flared up repeatedly. In the evening of June 23 about 160 men, women and children were standing in the Friedrich-Engels-Platz—the town was still under martial law and the assembly of more than three people was forbidden. A People's Police patrol fired a dozen rounds; the crowd scattered. A woman stood her ground: at her feet a thirteen-year-old boy lay dead.

4

The employees of the Zeiss optical instruments factory at Jena
had long been bitter opponents of the regime: nationalisation,
the collective wages contracts and other Communist favours
had robbed them of valuable benefits and privileges granted
many years before by the firm's enlightened founders, Carl
Zeiss and Ernst Abbé.

It was the Zeiss employees who led the rising in Jena on
June 17. Supported by men from the Schott glass⟍works, from
the railway repair yards and from the pharmaceutical factory,
they marched through the town, cleared out the offices of the
trades union movement and of the Communist youth organisa⟍
tion and broke into the local headquarters of the Society for
Sport and Technics, where they emptied the armoury and
smashed the rifles against the walls. At the SED headquarters
a detachment of armed police was waiting. Their position was
hopeless, however; within two minutes pamphlets, pictures,
records and card indexes were being flung out of the windows.
As in every other large town on that day, the demonstrators
made next for the prison. There was no resistance; as the great
iron gates gave way to the strikers' crow⟍bars, the police guards
hastened to open the cells and about a hundred prisoners, dazed
and blinking at the unaccustomed light, stumbled out into the
arms of the crowd outside. At that moment, police reinforce⟍
ments arrived in an open truck and an officer, the first to jump
down, fired his pistol, wounding two children. A dozen

strikers hurled themselves at him; others went for his men, most of whom escaped in various stages of undress into the Red Army military hospital opposite. There the Russian patients were leaning perilously from the windows, alternately cheering the mêlée below them and the spectacle a few yards up the street, where the pupils of a secondary school for girls were busily shovelling Communist literature, placards and a reproduction of the Peoples' President into the street.

Three hundred yards away another crowd had broken into the security police headquarters. But there were no prisoners to be freed: they had been taken away early that morning. In the basement the strikers found a water cell—a small stone cabin, the size of a domestic shower-bath, with a number of open-ended pipes through which cold water could be made to flow. They also found the chief of the Jena Security Police, Hauptmann Strauss. He was subsequently admitted into hospital.

Meanwhile, Russian troops had re-occupied the SED head-quarters and had arrested eight of the demonstrators. By 3 p.m. 25,000 people had massed in the square outside the building and were shouting for the men's release. More Russian troops arrived. Ignoring them, the strikers brought up a ladder and climbed to a second-storey window where they found one of the men handcuffed in a locked room. With difficulty he was brought down. The Russians closed in, using rifle-butts. Tanks appeared at the fringe of the square. But the crowd refused to budge. Women sat down in rows and forced the drivers to stop. Advancing from another angle, the tanks found their way blocked again—five trams had been abandoned in the square and the strikers pushed them together to form a barricade. Again and again the Russians, manoeuvring their tanks with difficulty, tried to break through: each time the strikers placed the trams across their bows. The game went on for fully half an hour before the tanks withdrew. Ten minutes later the tanks returned, this time approaching the square from three sides. The strikers rushed to their trams... but the Russians opened fire and the crowd scattered. Seconds afterwards the demonstrators realised that the Russians were firing over their heads. It was too late—the tanks had won.

A state of emergency was declared at 6 p.m. One after another, members of the strike committees were arrested, until 500 people were crammed into the cellars of the central police station where they had to lie, without bedding or food, on a stone floor. Next morning it was announced that the 26-year-fold "Western agent" Alfred Diener, a motor mechanic, had been sentenced to death by a Russian military court and shot.

At Apolda, June 17 began with a little ceremony outside the town hall. A tractor, a gift from the Soviet Union, was to be handed over to a State farm in the presence of Red Army officers. But the Party Secretary had scarcely begun his tribute to the generosity of "our Russian friends" when he was interrupted—not, as was usual on such occasions, by sustained applause but by whistling. Delighted, the crowd took up the refrain: "Ivan, go home!"—and, after removing the red flag from the town hall, went off home themselves. That evening factory workers from Jena led the townspeople to the local gaol to free the "politicals". But the building was already surrounded by Russian troops.

In Weimar, the employees of the locomotive works stopped work at 9 a.m. and elected a strike committee which included two directors. A resolution embodying the demands made by the Stalinallee building-workers on the day before was taken to the Town Hall with the request that it be forwarded to Berlin. The strike soon spread to other factories. Shortly afterwards, militarised units of the People's Police escorted by Russian armoured cars moved into the factories and, at the locomotive works, arrested the strike leaders, some of whom were later sent to prison. Although the strike continued until June 20, there was no demonstration in Weimar.

At Erfurt, the strike began at midday among the building-workers and a state of emergency was declared two hours later. Next day the news of the execution in Jena reached Erfurt—and the employees of three large factories joined the strike. Two of them were occupied by tanks; but the Russians made no attempt to break the strike. It continued until June 22.

5
Chemnitz is the name of Karl Marx Stadt · Why no rising in the uranium area? · Dresden: the strike goes on · Threats at Riesa

The news from Berlin reached "Karl Marx Stadt", as the Communists call Chemnitz, too late for demonstrations to develop. Although strikes broke out in a number of factories, too few sufficiently determined men came forward to lead them, and by June 19 the last strikers returned to work. The Soviet authorities declared a state of emergency nevertheless. On June 27 the Government arranged a mass "loyalty" demonstration in the market square: the entire population of the town was to take part and all those present were to put their names to a roll drawn up by the Party. Despite considerable pressure in the factories, only 3,000 people turned up—and all but a few of those who did so declined to sign the loyalty list: such a proceeding, they told Party officials was "not customary in a democracy".

What of the uranium mining area in the Erzgebirge, where tens of thousands of miners work night and day under the direction of the Russian "Wismuth" concern to supply precious raw material for the Soviet Union's atomic energy programme? For several weeks after the rising, rumours about a mass insurrection by the Wismuth miners spread through West Berlin and Western Germany. Whole regiments of People's Police were said to have been disarmed, there had been long and bloody battles with Soviet troops, 90 pits had been flooded. A clear picture did not emerge for a long time afterwards: in fact this was the one heavy industrial area which was scarcely involved in the rising. Yet it was the very part of the Soviet Zone where the spark from the Stalinallee might have been expected to act like a blazing torch in a hayloft; the Wismuth miners, working under the hardest possible conditions and housed in overcrowded barrack huts, were tough and had given trouble before. However, the reasons why they failed to play a major part in the rising are simple enough.

The German uranium area has long occupied Moscow's undivided attention; every part of the vast and sprawling Wismuth concern is under direct Russian control and is constantly guarded by Red Army units. The first sign of mutiny was bound to provoke the Russian authorities into immediate counter-action. Where attempts at strikes and demonstrations did occur they were almost invariably put down before they could gather momentum. Secondly, the news from Berlin was late to reach the uranium area. Thirdly, the men had no complaint about norms and wages: the uranium miners are still by far the highestpaid workers in the Soviet Zone, frequently earning three times the amount paid in other heavy industries. Nevertheless there were impressive attempts at resistance in several places and the Soviet authorities deemed it wise to declare a state of emergency throughout the mining area.

In Dresden, at the edge of the uranium belt, the strikers attempted to take over the central Post Office, with its important telephone and teleprinter exchange But the demonstration was slow to develop, and by the time the assault began at 2 p.m. the building was surrounded by a triple cordon of Soviet troops and German police. German officers formed the front rank, their men the second, Russian soldiers made up the third. And squatting formidably outside the main entrance was a T34 tank.

For many minutes demonstrators and police stood chest to chest, each side attempting to push the other back. Then a striker smashed his fist into a German officer's face. Uniformed men grabbed three of the demonstrators; the crowd tried to retrieve them; fighting broke out all along the line. The Russian Town Commandant, Colonel Bogdanov, arrived in the square and, using the town loudspeaker system, declared a state of emergency. The rising had scarcely started, however, and the crowd was still growing. At 5 p.m. a sizeable column of strikers from the outskirts tried to reach the centre of the town by crossing the Dimitrov Bridge, which was occupied by People's Police. Demonstrators and police eyed one another. "Be reasonable!", the strikers shouted. "Let's avoid bloodshed!" The police agreed and put their truncheons away. The strikers moved forward... but suddenly Russian troops arrived. Pushing the Germans aside and advancing with fixed bayonets they drove the strikers back.

That evening Russian troops turned Dresden into an armed camp; every factory of any size was occupied and tanks and machine-gun crews took up positions in the main streets and squares. Yet minor demonstrations continued until shortly before midnight.

Next day rumour had it that the whole of the Soviet Zone was in the grip of a general strike. Strikes broke out afresh where work had been resumed and 6,000 men at the Dresden electrical engineering works, who had worked throughout June 17, downed tools. At the extension to the Technical University building workers dropped their trowels and shovels and drew up a four-point resolution for transmission to Berlin. At 4 p.m. a thousand people returned to the square outside the Post Office. But the Red Army had declared martial law and was determined to enforce it—tanks divided the crowd, and infantry, using rifle-butts and firing warning shots into the air, chased the demonstrators into side-streets.

On June 19 Soviet troops occupied the Technical University building site and stayed there five days. State Security Service officials refilled the cells of the Police Praesidium and took over the exhibition hall as an overflow prison. Occasional shots could still be heard in the streets on June 21.

Riesa on the Elbe is celebrated for its steelworks, where nearly 9,000 men spend three-quarters of their working time on reparations orders for Soviet Russia. The steelworkers' strike began in the afternoon of June 16, as soon as they heard the news from the Stalinallee in Berlin. At 6 p.m. the men left the works;

when the night-shift did not appear for duty and the power system failed, the management was compelled to stop production. The strike continued throughout the seventeenth.

That evening Security Service officials, escorted by a detachment of militarised People's Police, arrested 150 strikers. But the early morning shift continued the stoppage, standing at their places of work but refusing to touch the machines. The strikers made known their demands: wages to be raised retrospectively; the present management to be withdrawn; the Government in Berlin to resign. At 7 a.m. the management gave orders for meetings in all departments; Party officials were to persuade the men to return to work. Refusal was unanimous. Three hours later the strikers staged a mass meeting in the works yard and empowered a committee to negotiate with the senior SED official in the factory, Comrade Friedemann. Friedemann was polite; he made detailed notes of the men's demands and announced that he would have to drive to Dresden to negotiate with representatives of the Government. The men agreed and Friedemann drove off, only to return at midday with a detachment of People's Police and two Red Army tanks. The building housing the strike committee was surrounded; the tanks trained their guns on the windows. Comrade Cempny, works manager and deputy Party Secretary opened the negotiations: "In my office next door there is a Russian officer," he said. "Tanks are in the yard. Have you any more to say?" But the strikers refused to give way. Cempny tried again: "Anyone not at work within 15 minutes will be arrested." Still there was no reaction from the strike committee. The Russian officer appeared: "All men refusing to work will be shot as provocateurs!" he shouted and police drove the men's representatives from the room. But the strike went on. At 1 p.m. the Minister for Foundry Construction, Selbmann, arrived at the steelworks. Broadcasting over the factory's loud-speaker system, he announced that those who wished to do so could go home. "Your factory passes will be taken from you at the gate and you can regard yourselves as dismissed. Anyone who remains on the premises but refuses to work will be arrested." Only a few men chose to go home; the remainder, cursing their own impotence, returned to work. The state of emergency was ended twelve days later.

6

The second Iron Curtain ⁄ "Frontier of friendship and peace" ⁄ Se-curity at Stalinstadt ⁄ Goerlitz: "Let's do things better ourselves" ⁄ Comrade Ehrlich provides a shield ⁄ "Old man Latt" and the Revo-lution of 1953 ⁄ "Ivan go home!"

We speak of the Iron Curtain and draw a line through north and central Germany, around the Czechoslovak frontier and past Hungary, Rumania and Bulgaria to the Black Sea; beyond it we imagine an empire stretching from the hills and plains of central Germany, across the forests of Poland and Russia, the steppes of Siberia, the Mongolian deserts and the Chinese rice-fields to the Pacific Ocean. We forget that behind the Iron Curtain that divides East from West, Europe from Europe Germany from Germany, are curtains of a texture at least as closely woven as the one we describe as "iron".

If the declarations of their leaders are to be believed, the Ger-man Democratic Republic and the "People's Republic of Poland", both of them provinces of the Soviet Empire, are united by bonds of the deepest friendship. It is true that the political beliefs of Russia's regents in Berlin and Warsaw are identical; they plan according to the same laws, think in the same terms, exercise the same principles and march in step to the command of the same master. The frontier they have drawn between one another they call a "Frontier of friendship and peace". But the citizen of Frankfurt-on-Oder is forbidden to cross the bridge and visit his Polish neighbour; nor may his Polish neighbour visit him. The frontier of peace is total and quiet as a grave. The individual provinces of the empire are isolation wards and what traffic there is between them is strictly controlled. In the Oder marshes, villagers occasionally meet a People's Police frontier patrol; sometimes they catch a glimpse of Polish guards on the opposite bank of the river; now and again they hear shots. That is all. News from the other side is rare. The German railwaymen who drive trains loaded with reparations goods through the Polish-administered part of Eastern Germany, through Poland itself and through the next curtain to Brest-Litovsk and who return with Russian ore and Polish coke—their scraps of news are meagre. The railwaymen unload their freight from the East at Fuerstenberg-on-Oder or, more accurately in Stalinstadt—"Germany's first Socialist town". Six blast furnaces wait there for raw materials, defying the basic economic law that iron and steel industries should be sited within reasonable distance of coal mines and iron ore. The Berlin planners, ignoring the tremendous additional freight costs involved, oblivious of the fact that their creation might at any moment be cut off from its raw materials, had resolved to construct a new steel town and call it Stalinstadt. At immense cost and after a succession of delays and breakdowns due to inept planning and frantic haste to announce completion by the Soviet leader's birthday, the blast furnaces were built. There were wildly celebrated successes; the launching of the first furnace was a national event of premier importance. And there were crises, affairs of bitter blame and abject self-criticism. The workers were driven hard because Soviet dogma of heavy industry as the only means to a higher standard of living demanded blind obedience. And why not? The planners' object was not to make a profit and there were eighteen million people to pay for the loss. There was often a shortage of coke; the planners conceived a grotesquely expensive method of using lignite in its place. The ventilation system broke down; men died of gas poisoning. But the furnaces functioned and if the men who served them had to live in cheerless and primitive temporary quarters, the Plan was being fulfilled—and that was what mattered. That the Housing Plan was not being fulfilled mattered not at all.

Here, too, in "Germany's first Socialist town" it was the building-workers who struck first. Early on June 17 they joined up with their colleagues at Fuerstenberg, beat up the trade union officials and demanded the abolition of working to norms, and called for lower prices, the resignation of the Government and freedom. And they marched—to Fürstenberg, where they stormed the town hall, fought with the police and were finally overpowered by Soviet troops, who appeared in larger numbers than in other towns. There were casualties, some of them fatal. In the steelworks only 800 men took part in the strike. There the regime was well equipped, both militarily and ideologically, to deal with the emergency: the blast furnaces were manned by "Youth Brigades", whose members were picked for their devotion to the cause; and Russian troops were on the spot by 10 a.m. They even searched the men's huts for weapons. In Frankfurt-on-Oder strikes broke out at building sites and in the railway repair yards. But when the men tried to demonstrate in the centre of the town they found strong Red Army contingents in occupation of every conceivable rallying place and, above all, guarding the approaches to the Oder Bridge and Poland.

Along almost the entire length of the "peace frontier" overt demonstrations seemed impossible. The one notable exception was at Goerlitz.

The larger part of this town lies on the western bank, the smaller part on the eastern bank of the river. The two are connected by a bridge. But the bridge is blocked and the river acts as a frontier: that is Goerlitz, where the Communist leaders signed the Treaty of Friendship defining the line of the Oder and Neisse rivers as Germany's permanent frontier with Poland. The Germans live on the western bank of the Neisse; on the eastern side are the Poles.

At the railway works in the Christoph-Luederstrasse the day-shift was due to begin work at 7 a.m. But the men stood about in groups, discussing the news they had heard on the radio. "If the Stalinallee people can do it, then so can we!" someone shouted. "Protest meeting! Outside—call the others!"

Half an hour later between two and three thousand men were on their way to the centre of the town. The news travelled quickly; one factory after another stopped work and by half past ten the men from the railway works were leading a small army. At the big H.O. department store on the Domianiplatz the sales girls fluttered to the windows and asked one another anxiously whether the men outside were coming to storm the shop. Then the truth dawned on them. Pausing only to run upstairs with the cash, the girls hurried into the street to catch up with the tail of the column. At the lower market square the strikers stopped outside a branch office of the State Security Service where they thought the mayor, Comrade Ehrlich, would be hiding. The shutters were closed and armed police in khaki stood guard behind them. Several youngsters climbed the face of the building, smashed a first floor window and called on the police to deliver the mayor. But he had already left the town, they were told. On to the town hall, to the hated man's office, where the contents of his desk flew from the windows together with his collection of signed photographs of the Leaders. Next door, the rank and file of the Communist youth organisation stormed the headquarters of their movement. Led by a young girl in the regulation blue blouse, they forced an entry and sent flags, posters and Marxist-Leninist literature raining down on the crowd below.

"Set the political prisoners free!" Taking up the cry which was ringing through a dozen other towns at that moment, the demonstrators hurried off to the prison, where more than a hundred of their fellow-citizens were undergoing interrogation before trial—most of them farmers in arrears with their deliveries and tradesmen who were unable to pay their taxes. Too surprised to resist, the prison guards were quickly disarmed and after welders from the railway works had opened the first cell they willingly unlocked the rest. Outside, a truck drew up; twenty armed policemen had arrived to restore order. The crowd moved threateningly, barring their way. Then a man who was to play a leading part at a later stage of the rising, an

architect, stepped forward. To try to intervene would be to in-
vite trouble, he told the police. They would be wise to hand
over their arms and go home. The policemen agreed, and did so.

At their next target, the headquarters of the SED, the strikers
found the most important man in Goerlitz, the Party's District
Secretary, Comrade Weichold. Weichold was badly beaten
up and made to march on with the crowd to the Security
Service headquarters where the occupants had prepared for a
siege. The great steel shutters were in position; a massive cupboard reinforced the door. But the strikers were not to be put
off so easily. Men with sledge-hammers and crow-bars closed
in and the barricades began to creak. Then shots rang out—the
SED men were firing over the heads of the crowd. One of the
demonstrators grabbed Comrade Weichold and, using him as
a shield, advanced towards the gate. Forced to negotiate, the
SED officials agreed to allow ten of the strikers into the building
to look for political prisoners. All had been removed but one
—a young People's Policeman who had been admitted a day
earlier. He was released. In the street, however, he was mistaken
for an SED official and was roughly handled by the crowd
before he could be rescued. Meanwhile, six of the strikers who
had returned to the basement to investigate a supposed tunnel
connecting the building with Russian garrison headquarters,
found that the cellar doors had been locked behind them.
By beating at a small grating, they managed to attract the attention of the crowd. Furious now, and forgetting that the officials
inside were armed, the strikers hurled themselves at the
entrance. A Security Police official opened fire—and awoke
hours later in hospital, fortunate to be alive. After five minutes
the six imprisoned strikers were released. The SSD paid

heavily; their offices were ransacked and all documents—including an impressive card-index system recording the political reliability of the citizens of Goerlitz, was destroyed.

Towards midday upwards of twenty thousand people collected in the market square, where technicians among the strikers had connected microphones to the town's loudspeaker system. The architect, a striker from the railway works, an employee of the Goerlitz optical factory, a publican, a tradesman and a town council official addressed the crowd in turn. Several days later the government was to describe the speakers as "fascist provocateurs, criminals and bandits" and to allege that they had incited the crowd to sabotage and violence. The reverse was the case. The architect set the tone of the meeting. "The Government", he said, "must resign. But we don't want to waste time talking about the mistakes of the past; those who are guilty will have to account for themselves in the regular courts. Instead, let's look ahead, keep together and resolve to do things better ourselves." At this moment the crowd made a lane for a group of strikers who had found the Communist mayor, Ehrlich. He was brought to the tribune and placed in front of the microphone. Visibly trembling—this was not the moment for a speech about the Five Year Plan or the Construction of Socialism—Ehrlich began: "In my opinion..." But the crowd had lost interest in the mayor's opinion and Ehrlich was pushed from the platform to make way for the election of a central strike committee of twenty men to take over his affairs. Calling another mass meeting for 3 p.m., the strike committee left for the Hotel Schwarzenberg in order to work out a plan of campaign.

The mass meeting over, a section of the crowd set off for the women's prison at the Postplatz. Here the guards put up a half-hearted defence with fire hoses; when these proved ineffective, they fired their rifles over the demonstrators' heads. No one was hit, however, and a dozen men battered at the gates with axes and heavy hammers until they gave way. A short sprint across the yard and the strikers had reached the cell block. The police continued to resist; but the strikers had learned the technique of liberating prisoners by now, and the cells were quickly opened. Wearing prison clothing, some four hundred women streamed out into the square. One of them, white-haired and thin, was serving a six years sentence for economic crimes: she had bought coffee in West Berlin.

At 3 o'clock the demonstrators returned to the market square and, when this was full, overflowed into the Postplatz and the Wilhelmplatz, where they followed the meeting over the loudspeaker system. An elderly working-man caught the mood of the crowd. "Friends," he cried, "I'm old man Latt. Since 1904 I have been a member of the Social Democratic Party. I've taken part in three revolutions—in 1918, in 1945 and now in the revolution of the seventeenth of June, 1953. I want to say that it is the joy of my life that I have been able to see this day. For eight years we have been bound and gagged; for eight years we haven't been able to say what we think. Now it's all over and we're free. We don't even need an election— anyone with eyes and ears can see and hear for himself what the people of the Zone have decided. Their vote is unanimous: the SED in Berlin and everywhere else must get out before the wrath of eighteen millions hits them. People of Goerlitz, long live the revolution of 1953!"

It was not a political speech, but it was what the crowd

wanted to hear. Whether old Socialists or ex-Nazis, whether
former Communists, intellectuals, working-people or tradesmen—all of them had wanted to say just what 'old man
Latt' had said.

His speech was the climax of the meeting; already the
revolutionary tide was beginning to ebb. Nobody knew what
the next few hours would bring. Rumour had it that in the
eastern part of the town the Poles were on the streets; that some
of them had swum across the Neisse. People claimed to have
seen them and even to have spoken to them: "Carry on,"
the Poles had said, "we'll help you, we'll send you weapons."

Four p.m. There were reports that strong formations of
People's Police and Soviet troops were marching on Goerlitz.
This was more than a mere rumour. Shortly before 5 p.m. an
armoured car halted at the edge of the square. Shrill whistles
from the crowd and chants of "Ivan go home!" Two People's
Police troop-carriers appeared—and were promptly surrounded.
Backing hurriedly, the trucks retired.

But it was now clear that the Government, far from acknow-
ledging its defeat, was preparing to counter-attack. At 5.30 the
SED, again in control of the loudspeaker system, announced
that the Russian Town Commandant had declared a state of
emergency: the assembly of more than two people was forbidden and offenders would be punished under martial law...
So the Red Army was to intervene. Until now they had
tolerated the rising, seemingly content that the workers should
overthrow the SED. At no time had the demonstrators become
involved with the occupation troops. Speaker after speaker had
warned against provoking the Red Army into taking action
and no one had contradicted them. And yet the Russians had

come to the Government's rescue after all. At 7 p.m. the demonstrators heard the sound of marching—disciplined, rhythmic marching now. Looking straight ahead and ignoring the crowd's abuse, two companies of barrack-based People's Police were marching with fixed bayonets through the Berliner Strasse. The SED announcer returned to the microphone: "People of Goerlitz, the People's Police now marching through the town have come for your protection. They have come to protect your places of work from fascist provocateurs and agents." Jeers and laughter greeted the announcement. But the threat was unmistakable.

Light tanks and police troop-carriers patrolled the town. Then, at dusk, the walls began to vibrate with the sound that had accompanied the last days of the Third Reich: ten T 34 tanks pushed through the narrow streets—to save its Quislings, the occupying Power was using the tanks that had saved Stalin-grad. But the Russians' rôle was strictly defensive; they avoided incidents and were remarkably indulgent. The larger crowds had broken up, but small groups of people stayed in the streets, ignoring the curfew.

The counter-revolution began before midnight. Driving at speed through streets they had not dared to tread a few hours before, the Security Police hunted out their victims. Had all been in vain? Had the West failed to understand the signal? What had happened in Berlin—and in other towns?

The strike continued next day. At the railway works alone, seventy men had been arrested and their mates refused to resume production until they were released. Scraps of news began to circulate. Mayor Ehrlich was firmly in the saddle again. Yester-day afternoon he had promised to resign: that evening he had toured the town, laughing at the strikers from the safety of a Russian armoured car. The strikers had formed a short-lived provisional administration; a doctor was to be the new mayor and the architect his deputy. There was also news from the schools. In four elementary schools the pupils had refused to work. Pictures of Party leaders had been ripped from the class-room walls; "Young Pioneers" who objected were thrashed; many of the teachers had joined the demonstrators. In the Goerlitz secondary school the pupils had elected a committee and had drawn up a list of demands—two teachers, both of them loyal members of the Party, must be dismissed; the FDJ was to be forbidden to intervene in academic affairs; the Society for Sport and Technology must be entirely excluded from the school; history teaching must no longer be adapted to suit Communist theory; Russian must no longer be a compulsory subject. Next day SSD men called at the school and arrested five of the boys. A few days later they were released and fled to West Berlin.

On June 20 work was resumed in the factories. Some of the men were dispirited, believing that oppression would now increase; others maintained that the SED would never recover from its defeat.

7

The coastal belt ⁄ "Fish instead of meat" ⁄ A launching postponed ⁄
Ulbricht's Navy moves in ⁄ Fortified Ruegen ⁄ Warnemuende: deadlock
at the dockyard gates ⁄ A losing battle from the start

Several years ago an American newspaper correspondent vi-sited one of West Berlin's many overcrowded refugee camps. He conversed somewhat hurriedly with one or two of the

6. BERLIN, JUNE 17: DEMOLISHING SECTOR BOUNDARY SIGN

7. BERLIN, JUNE 17: DASH FOR COVER BEFORE SOVIET ARMY SALVOES

8. BERLIN, JUNE 17: STONES *versus* TANKS

inmates and, looking for a pithy lead to his story, asked a housewife to sum up everyday life in the Soviet Zone in as few words as possible. The good woman, the story goes, gazed for a moment at the floor, looked up and said simply: "Fish instead of meat..." Perhaps only people with close personal experience of life within the Soviet orbit could be expected to understand the significance of her remark. It has been said that the most unmistakable characteristic of the Communist State is the penetrating smell of fish—particularly of herring—in all houses, alleys, railway trains and offices of the authorities, whether in Chemnitz, Lublin or Minsk. This is no criticism of fish; it is a criticism of the unshakable deter-mination of the Planners to wean humanity from meat. In the Soviet Zone the routine never changed: month by month and year after year they found themselves obliged to honour the meat ration coupons with fish—generally herrings. The fish was seldom fresh, but it was better than nothing. And the people ate; they were even grateful.

It was fitting that on June 18 the nationalised ship-yard at Stralsund was to launch a lugger, a vessel to be used by the herring fleet and to be given the name "Walter Ulbricht". The ceremony did not take place. One of the first acts of the night-shift on the evening before was to cover the name on the bow with thick black paint. When the early morning shift arrived, the men elected a strike committee and resolved to leave the dock-yard in a body. Pushing past a police guard of 20 men, the strikers poured through the gates—only to be brought to a halt by a cordon of Soviet troops with sub-machine guns at the ready. Should they risk a charge? At 7 a.m. Russian tanks appeared, to be greeted by the strikers with shouts of "So this is German-Soviet friendship!" The Russians posted machine-guns; one covered the dock-yard gates, the other the railway goods yard opposite. For several hours the two sides stood facing one another: the Russians, determined to prevent a demonstration yet anxious to avoid bloodshed; the men from the ship-yard, reinforced now by dockers and building-workers, stubbornly refusing to obey repeated injunctions broadcast over the yard's loudspeaker system to return to their places of work. At 10 o'clock three armoured cars and another company of Russian infantry arrived: using the butts of their rifles, the Russians forced the strikers back to the yard entrance. A group of SED officials, escorted by a Russian and a German officer, attempted to negotiate with the men, promising to lift the siege as soon as work was resumed. But the men refused; this was a German affair, they insisted, and the strike would go on until the last Russian soldier had been withdrawn. And they decided to attempt a mass break-out when the afternoon shift arrived at two. At one o'clock a strong formation of Sea Police moved in. Flanked by armoured cars and firing both live and blank ammunition, "Ulbricht's Navy" forced the strikers back while Russian troops held off the afternoon shift. Negotiations were re-opened. The strikers were allowed to leave the dock-yard in small groups and the afternoon shift to take their places. These promptly took the only course still open to them and declared a sit-down strike.

Since 1945 stretches of the Baltic coast had been declared prohibited areas, with road-blocks and barbed wire entangle-ments protecting a chain of military and naval bases from Wismar to Stettin. One of these was the island of Ruegen, once a celebrated resort and now the scene of vast and costly construction projects; coastal fortifications, a canal and a great new port to be called "Peace Town" were being built by thousands of labourers working under Russian direction. There was also a small army of slaves: at Glowe 5,000 political prisoners aged between fifteen and sixty were housed in camps surrounded by live wire and guarded by police who bore every resemblance to the concentration camp guards of the S.S. But late in the afternoon of June 17 the guards became friendly: there were rumours of a rising in Berlin and of the overthrowal of the Government.

In the camps occupied by the regular building-workers there were radios. That evening the men listened to the news bulletins from West Berlin, hearing with amazement of the rising, of its suppression by the Red Army, and learning that the capital was in the grip of martial law. Few of the men on Ruegen slept that night. Next morning they downed tools, elected strike committees and posted pickets. Then they set off for Glowe, intending to release the slave labourers. But the prison camp was surrounded by Soviet troops and the plan had to be abandoned. Returning to their own area, the building workers stormed the administrative buildings, ransacked the drawing office and, before the People's Police garrison could be summoned from Prora, destroyed blue-prints and files. Late that evening, after a state of emergency had been proclaimed throughout the island, two thousand East German soldiers restored some semblance of order, opening fire and driving the men into their barrack huts. The strike continued, however. On June 20, the Soviet authorities began dismissing the building workers; a few days later the political prisoners were removed to the mainland and the hutted camps dismantled.

Work on the great new base at Ruegen had come to a halt.

In the course of June 16 there appeared on one of the notice boards at the Warnow ship-yard in Warnemuende a docket which differed from all the customary notices that appeared there day after day, in that it was read. The notice set out a list of demands: that all increases in working norms be cancelled, that H.O. prices be reduced, that the worker's railway ticket be restored, that free and secret elections be held forthwith. Surprisingly, it remained on the board until June 18, on which day Warnemuende followed Berlin. The strike began in the machine shop and quickly spread; an hour later, work had stopped throughout the yard. Following the example of their colleagues in countless factories on the day before, the strikers ripped crude propaganda posters from the walls, dismantled the red star of Soviet Russia over the main gate and, after a brief struggle, disarmed the works police. At 8 o'clock the bulk of the first shift, a total of 12,000 men, tried to march to the centre of the town. But Soviet troops with fixed bayonets barred the way. In a clash two Russians were beaten up, and the arrest of two strikers followed. The soldiers pressed forward but the strikers held their ground, refusing to withdraw until the arrested men were released. An hour later the two men were handed over; but the strikers, still refused to budge. Two hundred People's Police—most of them non-commissioned officers—arrived and, shooting over the demonstrators' heads, managed to advance as far as the yard gates. But the strikers closed their ranks again—and drove the police back. Tanks, supported by 500 Russian infantrymen, finally broke the men's resistance. The second shift arrived at 2 p.m. and seeing the yard occupied by Soviet troops, turned on their heels and tried to organise a demonstration in the town. It was too late. Each time a crowd collected, the Red Army attacked, finally arresting more than a hundred of the strikers. For days on end tanks and light artillery guarded the approaches to the harbour, the main streets and, in particular, the road leading south to Rostock, where the ship-yard and building-workers had demonstrated and clashed with People's Police on June 17. Here unrest continued for several days; as late as June 20 the trawlermen, furious that the Navy, far from leading the revolt as in 1918, had let the revolutionaries down, had rows in dockside pubs with members of the Sea Police.

On maps which attempt to give a geographical picture of the rising, the symbols representing strikes and demonstrations are concentrated round Berlin and in the southern half of the Soviet Zone; across the wide plains of Mecklenburg and New Brandenburg in the north the marks of revolution are scattered and few in comparison. Only the Baltic ports are starred and underlined—yet here, too, the rising failed to develop, soon breaking down in face of the obstacles placed in its way. The reasons for this are plain. A popular rising needs the masses; it can only succeed in a closely populated area, in an industrial region. Secondly, the news from the capital reached the northern towns a day too late. By the time the alarm had been received, understood and translated into action, the regime and its protectors were prepared; the rebels fought a losing battle from the start. If in East Berlin, in Brandenburg, Magdeburg, Goerlitz and in the industrial area around Halle and Leipzig the workers had a brief opportunity to seize power, in the north

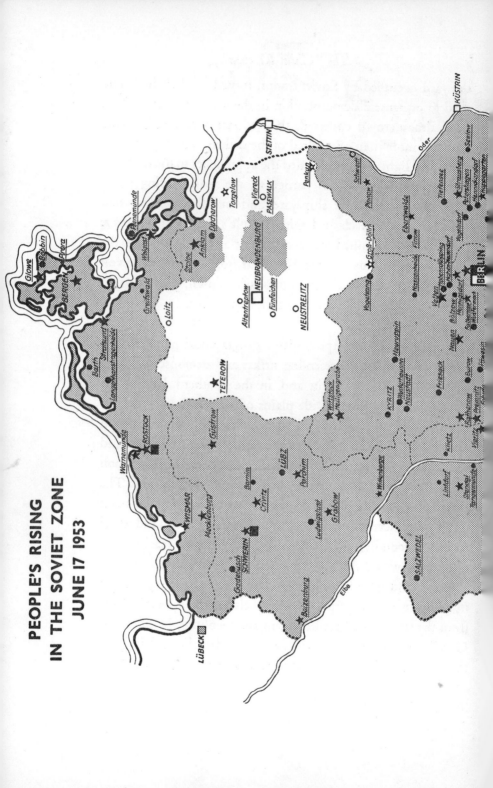

PEOPLE'S RISING
IN THE SOVIET ZONE
JUNE 17 1953

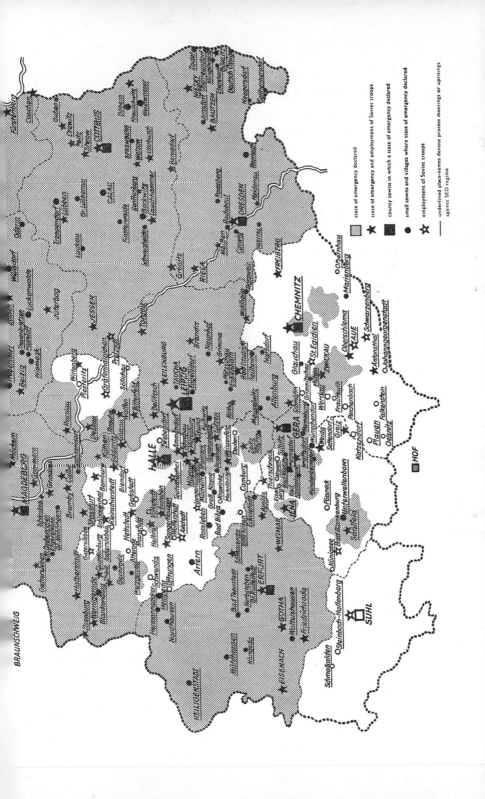

the opportunity did not present itself for a single moment. The ship-yard workers were not to know this; they were acting instinctively, obeying an irresistible summons to protest. All they could hope for was to win a single day of freedom and the respect of the myrmidons of the law, and the chance to prove that the slave-drivers and petty dictators for their part had failed to conquer a yard of territory in their eight years' battle against resistance. This was proved—not only in the ports, but in almost every other town in this calm and sleepy region. There were strikes in Boitzenburg on the Elbe—as late as June 19 the Russians were obliged to secure the market square with four heavy tanks. There were strikes at Ludwigslust. In Grabow the citizens held a mass meeting, chased the mayor out of town and beat up the District Secretary of the SED. In Schwerin the factories simmered for several days. At the Soviet airfield in Parchim a battalion of Russian troops was used to break a strike by building-workers. In Luebz sawmill workers declared a strike and marched on the town hall. At Guestrow the employees of an imprisoned furniture manufacturer marched on the gaol and demanded his release from custody. In Teterow two thousand industrial workers, farmers and private citizens demonstrated outside the municipal offices and the local gaol, and forced their way into the magistrates court. In Greifswald a strike of the railway maintenance men continued until June 23. At Anklam employees of the sugar factory, the furniture factory and of the machinery and tractor stations downed tools and cleared their places of work and the streets of the town of Communist propaganda posters. Farmers and farm labourers from surrounding villages streamed into the town to make their demands and to register their protest against the regime.

CHAPTER IX

THE FARMERS' REVOLT

Sixteenth-century class struggle ⁄ Disturbances of the peace and rioting ⁄ Revolt at Schlossrippach ⁄ Thansgiving at Sachsendorf ⁄ Jessen and the imprisoned farmers ⁄ Factory worker and farmer shoulder to shoulder

THE PARTY OFFICIAL IN THE TOTALITARIAN STATE IS required to be beadle and secret policeman, non-commissioned officer and foreman—above all, schoolmaster. For the Party, the "great teacher of peoples", is the ever-extended forefinger, instructing and threatening and always knowing best. The Party lays down how to build bridges, cut costumes, plant potatoes; it awards marks for their essays to writers, scolds composers for their symphonies, nags the philosophers and keeps an especially sharp eye on the historians. It rewrites the history of peoples at will, raising and lowering values to suit the current political line, turning heroes into criminals and lunatics into torch-bearers of wisdom.

One of the discoveries of the SED was Thomas Muenzer, the peasant leader, militant atheist and murdering firebrand of Zwickau. The Party resolved to grant Muenzer belated recognition as a sixteenth-century prophet of progress; his peasant rabble, it was decided, had borne the banner of revo-lution against feudalism and "early capitalism". In future he was to be regarded as one of the greatest sons of the German people. Muenzer was accordingly honoured in school-books, lectures were devoted to him in the Universities, factories and collective farms were dedicated to him. The Party saw to it that the farmers' ears rang with the rebel's name.

Perhaps the teachers in Berlin wondered later whether their pupils on the land had not learned the lesson too well. The seventeenth of June was not only the business of the industrial working-class and townspeople, but of the farmers and farm-labourers too. It would be too much to give to the hundred little storms in the villages the character of a rising; it would be more accurate to speak of disturbances of the peace and of rioting. Yet that is only half the story. The farmers were not able to record spectacular marches, impressive demonstrations or mass attacks on the citadels of power—but this was not their object. What mattered was that in a hundred places the farmers assembled while the workers were assembling, that they tried to join the workers, that they regarded the affair of the cities as their affair—that the rising of June 17 embraced all sections of the community, that eighteen millions rose as one. It was the whip of the norm that had driven the industrial worker onto he streets; in the farmer's case it was the delivery quota. For the farming community the load had become unbearable—we have described their troubles. Day after day the tax inspectors, quota commissars and dispossession squads hunted the farmers off their land; week after week hundreds were taken away for trial; the courts worked rapidly and savagely. Farming folk are conservative, respecting authority and taking time to make decisions; it takes a great deal of provocation to drive them into rebellion. But on June 17 the measure was brimming over.

In the village of Schlossvippach in Thuringia, two farmers were arrested on June 10. They were not the first, there was no reason to hope that they would be the last, and when they were dragged through the main street their children followed, crying. A dispossession squad was to requisition all tools, furniture and household goods belonging to the two men and their families. Neighbours arrived on the scene first, however, taking everything that could be moved to places of safety. Next day, the SED Press announced the "new course", enumerating the mistakes of the past in much humiliating detail. The farmers of Schlossvippach understood the Party jargon well enough; it was clear to them that the Government now thoroughly dis⁄approved of the arrest of their two friends. They consulted, went in a body to see the Mayor and demanded an immediate meeting of the inhabitants. The Mayor agreed and the villagers, summoned from fields and stables by bell and messengers, hurried to attend. The Party Secretary intervened to protest that the meeting was illegal; he was shouted down. One of the farmers took matters into his own hands. He telephoned to the public prosecutor at Soemmerda, told him that valuable acres were lying fallow and announced that if the two men were not released by two o'clock that afternoon, their friends would march over and fetch them. The prosecutor then promised their discharge. At 11 a.m. a People's Police squad car arrived. But the farmers, swinging rakes and forks as the followers of Thomas Muenzer had done 400 years before, threatened to crack the skull of any who dared to get out of the vehicle and the police retired. Next morning more police arrived from Soemmerda to arrest the farmers' spokesman; they found a cordon of men with clubs and pitchforks surrounding his farm. For several hours police and villagers faced one another, the farmers kept supplied with food and drink by their wives. Towards evening police reinforcements arrived and, after a short struggle, forced their way into the farm where they arrested the owner's wife—her husband was in hiding. But the two imprisoned men were released.

In the same week four farmers who had been imprisoned for "economic sabotage" returned to the nearby village of Eckel-stedt; all four were "kulaks" and, so the Party said, were detested by the smaller farmers as capitalists and exploiters of labour. They returned to a riotous welcome in a village street decorated with bunting and flowers, were given presents by their neighbours and were greeted by the rector with pealing church bells. To the north, the people of five villages near Sangerhausen arranged to demonstrate together. They did so, as late as June 19, but their demonstration was broken up by the police.

At a mass meeting in the village of Polleben, near Eisleben, twelve farmers announced their withdrawal from the collective farm "Thomas Muenzer". Not far away at Gerbstedt the villagers removed the red flag from a collective named after Ulbricht. At Soellichau the drivers and mechanics of the Machinery and Tractor Station went on strike, tore up their Party cards and caused a riot which had to be put down by Soviet troops. In Schafstadt, near Merseburg, the farmers attacked the collective farm "Friedrich Engels" and beat up the Party Secretary. At Domburg-on-the-Elbe, with a population of 900, the villagers decided to dissolve their collective. They removed the Mayor from his post and set about forming a "Free Movement"—its leaders were promptly arrested. The people of Wetterstedt, a hamlet of a hundred souls, attempted on June 18 to march to Quedlinburg to join up with the industrial workers—they were stopped by Russians at the outskirts of the town. Strikers from Magdeburg brought the news of the rising to Sachsendorf on June 17. The village teacher was charged with the task of drafting a summons to a mass meeting at 8 p.m.; his pupils carried the news on bicycles to neighbouring villages. In Sachsendorf itself, posters and flags were torn down and a delegation called on the local policeman to relieve him of his pistol. The constable promised to behave, however, and was allowed to keep it. In a packed village hall that evening several farmers spoke: the day of freedom had come at last; the Government must resign and there must be free elections; all political prisoners and prisoners-of-war still in the Soviet Union must be released immediately; measures must be taken to raise the standard of living. The local collective farm was declared dissolved and the heads of ninety families signed a formal statement of their demands. The Mayor, a Party member, announced his support for the villagers and was re-elected; a "revolutionary committee" was appointed to assist him. The villagers felt that the occasion was a great moment in their lives; before they went home they stood together and sang the old hymn, "Now thank we all our God".

At nearby Gnadau the villagers dissolved the collective farm "Friendship". At Loitsche the farmers, roused by strikers from Magdeburg, marched in a body to the Mayor's office and then deprived the local youth leader of his favourite toy, the only small-bore rifle in the village.

The farming community was no less active in the Brandenburg area. At Gross-Kreutz, for example, forty youngsters rushed up and down the main street, tearing placards from the walls and yelling abuse at the Communist authorities. Russian soldiers drove a truck into the middle of the band, snatched up a boy and demanded the names of the ring-leaders. Frightened but tight-lipped, he refused to speak. The Russians drove off, taking the boy with them. Still he refused to give his friends away. After a few miles the truck halted and an officer handed the boy a coin, telling him to nip off home. Next day officials went from house to house in an attempt to find the "fascist provocateurs". A week later the Party called a mass meeting to demonstrate the loyalty of Gross-Kreutz to the regime. Of 1,500 inhabitants, seven turned up.

At Fohrde, near Premnitz, youngsters took advantage of the confusion to beat up the Communist youth leader. At Briesen, near Nauen, the farmers thrashed the more bumptious Party officials. In the hamlet of Zodel, a few kilometres from Goerlitz, farmers roped together the Mayor, the head of the co-operative store, the director of the collective farm and the schoolmaster and made them dance at the head of a procession. They demolished the SED headquarters, smashed the small-bore rifles belonging to the FDJ and elected a new village council, arranging to sound the fire alarm in the event of an attack by police or Russian troops. The siren wailed at 10 p.m., and the villagers poured into the main street, barricading each end with farm carts. The police opened fire... seven men were arrested; six were later sentenced to terms of imprisonment ranging from six to 15 years.

The little market town of Jessen supports a Red Army garrison of 1,000 artillerymen as well as a detachment of People's Police. At 9 a.m. on June 17, 400 people collected in the market square and decided to march on the council offices. Two police sentries retired as the procession came in sight; the SED Secretary, the public prosecutor and other local government and Party officials appeared on a balcony. They shouted down to the crowd below that it should appoint a spokesman. The farmer who was chosen put forward four demands: the immediate release of all arrested farmers; reduction of the individual farmer's delivery quota to the level enjoyed by the collective; equitable distribution of fodder; strike pay for participating industrial workers. The district council chairman promised that the demands would be met within twenty-four hours; the public prosecutor added that the prison discharges had been unaccountably delayed and would take place forth-with. Accompanied by three of the demonstrators, the prosecutor drove off to Herzberg. At midday over 4,000 people met in the market square and set off on a tour of the town, carrying improvised placards and banners and shouting in chorus for the Government's resignation. Early in the afternoon the three delegates returned from Herzberg, bringing with them 23 released farmers. At 4 o'clock Russian tanks appeared and the Soviet Commandant declared a state of emergency.

It has not yet been possible to draw up a complete account of the disturbances in the villages on and after June 17; nor can we be certain of the extent of the agricultural community's gains. Everywhere the farmers' chief target was the collectives—we know that more than 400 collective farms were dissolved. We know, too, that to this day the Party has treated the farmer with greater respect. On the other hand, much of the old pressure on the individual has returned to the villages, regulations have become stricter again, arrests are frequent and the ominous slogan "class struggle on the land" has crept back into the Press. Nevertheless, June 1953 showed that farmers and workers found common cause, fighting together in direct contravention of the dogma which supposes the existence of "insurmountable class barriers" between agricultural labourers and peasant farmers, on the one hand and the "capitalist big farmer, or kulak", on the other. If there was a class struggle, it was the struggle of the privileged class of State and Party officials versus the rest. Every other barrier was wiped out.

9. Magdeburg, June 17: "Set the political prisoners free!"

10. BERLIN, JUNE 26, 1953: ZAISSER, ULBRICHT, GROTEWOHL AT SED "LOYALTY RALLY"

CHAPTER X

BAPTISM OF FIRE

People's Police versus People ⁄ Rearmament in stages ⁄ "Just and unjust wars" ⁄ "Imitation Russians" ⁄ The effect of Rising on the Red Army ⁄ Eight years old in 1945

AMONG SENIOR STAFF OFFICERS OF THE PEOPLE'S POLICE the seventeenth of June became known as the "great test". It was in fact the Soviet-German soldiers' baptism of fire; instead of shooting at cardboard targets they had fired on men and women, and the butts of their rifles had struck human backs instead of dummies of straw and sacking. Certainly Ulbricht's Red Army had passed its exam. The officers had imagined a different kind of test, of course. Though always enjoined to appear in public as policemen, among themselves and during "political study" with the troops it was customary to define their rôle bluntly: we are soldiers, they said. In January 1952 the Government had granted the People's Police the status of an "armed force of the Republic" charged with the honourable duty of defending the State against the internal and external enemy. The internal enemy was not taken very seriously; he could be left with confidence to the State Security Service. From the earliest days the drilling, marching, tactical and weapon training had been directed against "aggressors". The Soviet authorities, anxious to increase the strength of the satellite armies had wasted no time in preparing for the re-militarisation of their zone of Germany; in August 1946— before the Western occupation Powers had begun to consider centralising the executive powers of the newly formed West German *Laender* —a central police authority appeared in East Berlin under the name of "German Administration of the Interior". Two years later, in July 1948, the Russian authorities ordered the raising of militarised police formations in each of the five *Laender* of the Soviet Zone; known as *Bereitschaften*, they were placed under the command of "Chief Inspector" Hermann Rentzsch, a prisoner-of-war captured at Stalingrad. In October 1949 "Inspector-General" Wilhelm Zaisser assumed command; in the spring of 1950 Walter Ulbricht's Secretary, Heinz Hoffman, took over what was now known as the "Central Administration for Training". Senior Commands were entrusted to veteran Communists with experience of the Spanish Civil War and of Soviet military academies; lesser post were open to ex-officers and non-commissioned officers of the *Wehrmacht* who had given evidence of their ideological suitability as students at "*antifa*-courses" in Russian prisoner-of-war camps. One of the more prominent "anti-Fascist" students, Colonel von Witzleben (a nephew of Field Marshal von Witzleben, who was executed for his part in the July 1944 plot against Hitler) was given command of the officers' school at Kochstedt near Dessau. By the autumn of 1949 the *Bereitschaften* were organised in infantry, artillery, tank and engineer units with a Russian officer (in German uniform) attached to each, who was responsible for training. By November 1950 the force numbered 60,000. It was an Army in which officers and N.C.O.s predominated, a cadre to be expanded quickly by a recruiting campaign in time of need. Political instruction played a prominent part; "Polit-cultural" officers responsible for ideological training were allotted to each Company in the manner of the Red Army's political Commissars and the "National-Socialist leadership officers" of Hitler's *Wehrmacht*.

When the Communist army of North Korea crossed the 38th Parallel in 1950, the East German Government made preparations for a possible operation against the Federal German Republic. People's Police recruiting officers combed the factories, and the ranks began to fill with a new type of young soldier—politically indifferent, half pressed into service, half seduced by promises of considerable material advantages. From the date of his enlistment the recruit was compelled to break his ties with the West; he could neither write nor receive letters from the Federal Republic. The Party line decreed that he was to be brought up in "burning hatred of the imperialist warmongers" and to regard the Democratic Republic as the base for "the national war of German liberation". For this purpose he was instructed in the doctrine of just and unjust wars; he was taught that wars which served "progress" were just and that in determining the character of war such questions as which side attacked first and upon whose territory fighting took place were irrelevant. To remove any doubt, Inspector-General Hoffmann announced that any war which involved the Soviet Union against imperialist aggressors was "most deeply just" and that the People's Police would support such a war with all the strength at its command.

In January 1952 the Ministry of the Interior in East Berlin assumed the functions of a War Office—its responsibilities for "home affairs" were entrusted to a separate and subordinate department. A former Lieutenant-General of the *Wehrmacht*, Vinzenz Müller, became the Minister's first deputy and acted

as Chief of Staff; other deputies were Heinz Hoffmann as
G.O.C. Land Forces, Waldemar Verner as Chief of Sea
Police and Rudolf Doelling, Controller of Political Administration. (Shortly afterwards the air and naval forces were again
placed under the control of the Army). In January 1954 the
strength of the East German *Luftwaffe* was estimated at 5,000
officers and men, equipped with 50–60 Russian YAK jet
fighters and stationed in the area of Cottbus, Drewitz, Bautzen
and Kamenz. Rear-Admiral Verner's Sea Police consists of
10,000 officers and ratings and about fifty light patrol craft.
The army is divided into two major formations. Army Group
North, commanded by Major-General Rentzsch, has its headquarters at Pasewalk; Army Group South, at Leipzig, is
commanded by Major-General Vogel. In strength and organisation both resemble the Army Corps of the *Wehrmacht*: each
consists of two mechanised infantry divisions, an armoured
division, a regiment of field artillery, an anti-aircraft regiment,
an anti-tank regiment, an engineer battalion and signals
battalion. An armoured division is equipped with 225 T34
and Stalin 11 tanks, an infantry division with sixty-two tanks.

The total strength of the East German armed forces is put
at 125,000. In 1952 military ranks and badges were introduced,
the blue civil police uniforms were withdrawn and the army
issued with khaki uniforms cut on the Soviet pattern.

Thus it was that the strikers on June 17 found themselves
confronted by "imitation Russians" as the Berliners called
them—youngsters in loose-fitting khaki tunics, jackboots and
flat saucer-like caps pulled down over the eyes or forage caps
worn on one ear. At official ceremonies which had been held
up and down the country since the Second Party Conference of

the SED, the workers had had to present the young soldiers with rifles—"donations from the people", they were called. Now the seventeen-, eighteen- and nineteen-year-olds were to use the same weapons to fire on the same workers. They scarcely understood. But they had been trained to blind obedience and they fired when they were told to. And still they scarcely understood.

At short briefings late on June 16 the troops were told by their officers that they were to collect leaflets dropped by enemy aircraft; when instead of leaflets they found demonstrating workers, they were told that American agents had infiltrated into the Republic and stirred up sections of the population. The young soldiers accepted the story; they knew of more pleasant ways of spending their time than beating down unarmed civilians but orders had to be obeyed and discipline held them together. Behind them was the Red Army. Their own ranks were peppered with potential informers; the principal task of the "Polit-cultural" officer and the agent of the State Security Service was to build up a close network of stool-pigeons which could be relied upon to prevent the growth of a spirit of solidarity or even of comradeship among the men. Doubtless many of the youngsters would have preferred to throw down their rifles and march with the strikers and many must have wondered whether they were not fighting on the wrong side. But the distance from question to answer and from wish to fulfilment is far, and the obstacles facing those who would have liked to join the demonstrators were great. Where the People's Police appeared in small and isolated groups, however, the iron band of discipline sometimes gave way and there were notable cases of mutiny and laying down of arms. At

Halle a company commander of People's Police from the Loeberfeld Barracks near Erfurt ordered his men to drop weapons; he was arrested and later executed by a Red Army firing squad. The "Polit-cultural" officer of an infantry unit at Oranienburg refused to order his men to fix bayonets. He was court-martialled and reduced in rank. Similar cases were reported from Erfurt and Gera; there were signs of an attempted mutiny among Sea Police at Stralsund. In no garrison was, there an attempt at open rebellion, however; had one occurred, there is no doubt that counter-action by the Red Army would have been swift and terrible.

Resistance to the strikers among the "blue" civil police was much weaker. These were seldom difficult to disarm and in many cases showed sympathy with the rising—facts explained partly by their comparative isolation and partly by their local connections.

Many strong Red Army formations in Eastern Germany were on exercises when the demonstrations began and they were well prepared. This advantage was outweighed by the fact that the training locations were far from the industrial areas and centres of the rising. The troops themselves were well disciplined: with remarkably few exceptions they carried out orders scrupulously, avoiding bloodshed wherever possible. The small Russian guard units in the towns invariably did their utmost to keep clear of trouble, to the extent of sometimes abandoning their posts; the strikers' conclusion that the Red Army not only tolerated but actually approved of the demonstrations is understandable. And it may well be that the sympathetic gestures by individual Russian soldiers living in daily contact with the Germans were genuine. The larger units

of the Red Army are completely isolated, on the other hand;
throughout their term of service in Germany the men live in
camps and barracks as virtual prisoners. Nevertheless, in several
cases members of large Russian formations showed great reluctance to open fire on the strikers; a Russian emigré organisation
in Berlin has reported that 18 Soviet officers and men were
executed after June 17 for refusing to obey orders.

What was the simple Russian private to make of the rising?
Though his superiors did their best to satisfy his curiosity with
the usual phrases about "fascist provocateurs" and "American
Imperialist plots", on the streets he could see for himself. The
demonstrators were the same men and women who had been
liberated by his comrades from slavery and misery in 1945,
who had been showered by Mother Russia with the blessings
of Progress and Socialism, who for the first time in their
country's history had been given a People's and Workers'
Government. And now the people had risen against their
government, driven by cares and needs remarkably similar
to the cares and needs of his own people at home. Although
a spontaneous reaction from the Russian soldier was too much
to expect, his head must have reeled with questions and
doubts—and with these he returned to camp and finally to the
depths of Soviet Russia. The inquirer after the impact of
the June rising on the Red Army would do well to consider,
not the immediate reaction but the aftereffects.

Summer 1953 was a season of rumours. The West German
Press bristled with wild speculation about the consequences of
the rising and the future of the "new course". There were reports of drastic cuts in the strength of the People's Police; in
fact, about 10,000 men were discharged (and replaced by new

recruits). Unreliables, doubters, refractory elements or incom-
petents were sent home and the cadre closed its ranks, retaining
an élite that was undeniably dangerous.

It would be a mistake to see in every People's Policeman an
ardent Communist, the bearer of a message. The fanatics are
in the minority and East Berlin will never succeed in changing
this. He is for the most part a new type of mercenary; we may
encounter him in any West Berlin camp for People's Police
deserters. In very few cases are political motives the cause of the
young soldier's desertion—any more than political convictions
were the stimulus which caused him to enlist. In fact, both entry
and exit constitute escape, whether into barracks or out of
their gates for ever.

The eighteen-year-old recruit of today was eight years old
in 1945. His childhood meant war, it meant the collapse of
material and spiritual values, it meant robbery, murder and
petty theft, it meant hunger. He grew up knowing only
uniformity and spiritual strangulation, against a background
of oppression, poverty and lies. The same generation in
Western Germany enjoyed the inestimable advantage of
experiencing the beginning of a sound and lasting way of life.
Their cousins in the Soviet Zone were brought up in a period
of cold revolution and in surroundings which gave them no
opportunity to strike roots, or to learn and recognise true values.
This is their greatest difficulty; it is also their greatest danger.
Largely helpless, they hesitate between two poles—between the
small class of young Communist activists and the much larger
class of young people with the will to resist the regime. This
kind of flotsam is classic raw material for cannon-fodder, never
questioning the justice and morality of an order, not concerned

with war aims, merely obeying and fighting—so long as it seems to pay. But does it pay in a real emergency? Is it still worth while, not only when defenceless demonstrators are to be beaten into submission but when open battle against a highly trained and well equipped army imposes a genuine trial? Nowhere is the answer better known than in the Soviet headquarters at Karlshorst,—and none fear it more than the leaders of the SED.

CHAPTER XI

EIGHTEEN MILLIONS MAKE HISTORY

Power without authority · Loss of face in East Berlin · If the life-line parts · Inquisition, accusation and counter-accusation · Class conscious- ness mislaid · Search for scapegoats · Contact with the masses · Passive resistance · The pride of colleague Bremse · "Butter, not guns" · Freedom of discussion? · The "new course" abroad · Fall of Beria · Struggle for power in East Berlin · The Zaisser-Herrnstadt plot · Ulbricht at the helm again · Beria's foreign policy and the Red Army · Renewed hopes after Geneva Conference · Dilemma of East German leaders · Oelsner tries to set the clock back · Failure of recruiting cam- paign · Secular "consecration ceremonies" · Greifswald students rebel · Church versus State · Need to boost German Democratic Republic

IT HAS BEEN REPORTED THAT THE CHAIRMAN OF THE SED organisation in Berlin, Comrade Hans Jendretzsky, collapsed with a nervous breakdown on June 17. Nothing could illus- strate better the state of mind of the Party leaders on that day. After the rising had been crushed, they found themselves ignored by their Russian masters and left alone in benumbed and tottering confusion. The Comrades were disposed to greet the intervention of the Soviet tanks as their salvation; in reality, the presence of Russian soldiers in East Berlin, Brandenburg, Magdeburg, Halle, Goerlitz, Dresden and countless other towns and villages bore witness less to the defeat of the eighteen millions than to their own impotence. In proclaiming a state of emergency the Red Army had been forced to divest its East Berlin puppets of power and to expose to the gaze of the world the emasculation of the men for whom Moscow had forged the stirrup, whom they had lifted into the saddle and supported with dogged patience since 1946. To the people of the Soviet Zone it was confirmation of what they already knew: after seven years in command the Red republicans were still dependent on power lent them by their protectors. But lasting domination depends less upon power than upon authority; power demands constant submission, and submission can quickly turn to mutiny. Authority requires and is granted respect, which in time of trouble and unrest is confirmed in willing obedience.

The Soviet authorities, then, had been compelled to rob their German deputies of even the semblance of legitimacy and credit. It was a loss that could never be regained. Even more serious, the German Communists had lost face where their Russian overlords were concerned. In a world ruled according to the principle that the legitimacy of an action is in direct proportion to its success, failure is criminal. The conception of sin has been uprooted in the Soviet orbit; there is error, refusal, weakness and crime. But the catalogue of Communist offences cannot entirely hide the fact that the notion of sin, stripped of its religious implications and rationalised, remains. Hell-fire flares in *this* world, however, not in the next; in the Communist sphere the questionable assertion that all guilt is punished on Earth has become simple and terrible reality—with dictators deciding what is sin and what constitutes guilt. Those who become their followers expose themselves to the law of permanent inquisition—none knows this better than the lesser Communist leader.

Which, then, was the SED official to fear more: trial by the people or trial by the Party? Only this double threat can explain the hopeless disorder within the SED after the rising. For Party Secretaries at factory, town, district and county levels, for Walter Ulbricht himself, it was impossible to discover what in a given situation was the right course or the wrong, what was justifiable and what was not. The thin red thread of the Party line weaves its way through the years, and it is the Communist's most sacred duty to keep a firm grip on it. But what if the lifeline suddenly snaps?

On the seventeenth of June the Comrades were like children who set out to explore a cave and lose their lamps—or like moles, chased from their tunnels and exposed to the searing glare of daylight. What were they to do, for there was no one to tell them? Where were they to go, for there was none to point the way? They had not yet recovered from the nightmare of the previous week, when all their stern and zealous measures on the Party's behalf were condemned as wrong, bad and wicked in the "new course". They had merely grasped that according to the inscrutable decrees of their leaders, caution, compliance and even friendliness were required. But how far, they had asked themselves, should they go? On June 17 the question had come to this: how far might the Party functionary retreat in face of a rebellious populace? The norms were reduced; that much was clear—East Berlin had said so, following the march of the Stalinallee building workers on June 16. But what then? The Politbureau, proclaiming the "new course", had said something about wrongful arrests and unjust prison sentences: were political prisoners to be released when industrial workers and farmers demanded it? Were strikes to be recognised? Was it permitted to negotiate with the strikers' representatives? Or was this irresponsible, disloyal, weak and criminal? There was no answer for the tortured little Comrades. It was a long time, too long for some, before headquarters replied—with tanks and machine-guns.

Most rank-and-file Party members took the obvious and simple course, joining the demonstrators with whom they belonged. Party members in minor posts did likewise. For hundreds of thousands of nominal Communists and reluctant fellow-travellers, it was the day of vindication; many did not hesitate to rip Party badges from lapels and throw away the "most precious document of their lives", their Party membership books. For the senior official the decision was harder. When in doubt, he had no choice but to defend the ideals which he himself, perhaps, no longer shared, and to oppose a force which he too perhaps respected. If he were to yield, the Party would reckon with him; if he were to stand fast, the strikers would do so. It was the Party, however, which supplied not only his convictions but his generous share of daily bread.

According to the rules of the totalitarian State, the "new course" should have been followed, as all such radical changes in the Party line are followed, by a purge. The seventeenth of June, however—if Stalinist logic were still worth anything at all—deserved a mass inquisition. There was no delay; the post-mortem followed the rising with the speed, it seemed, of sound. Thousands who had pretended to be devoted sons of the Party had prostrated themselves before the "class enemy"; even the truly faithful had fallen. For the first few weeks after the rising, the Comrades were so busy providing reciprocal proof of how ignominiously they had failed to stand up to the great test that they all but forgot the crimes of the "fascist provocateurs". A Party newspaper in Dresden commented on the extraordinary frequency of missing SED badges since June 17: "Evidently the pins have lost their nerve, simply breaking off or slipping out of the lapel together with the badges. The latter, for their part, seem to have agreed to remain in hiding. Badges of the German-Soviet Friendship Society, or Karl Marx medallions, might be worn instead—but these have also disappeared. As for the trades union movement badges, these are virtually extinct. It would seem that Party leaders should help these Comrades to find their missing badges and mislaid class-conciousness without delay."

The Party leaders were occupied with their own mislaid class-conciousness. The inquisition opened. For the present, insofar as they had not been handed over the to State Security Service as strike leaders, the rank-and-file members were ignored; the first to be called to account were waverers in the intermediate positions. The Chief of Police in the Magdeburg area was held responsible for the storming of the city's Police Praesidium and was dismissed from his posts in police and Party. The First Secretary of the Party organisation in the Buna chemical works, Comrade Rinkel, was sacked for his failure to detect the presence in the factory of a "strong fascist under-ground movement", and because some of his subordinates in the Party had allowed themselves to be "seduced by the provo-cateurs". A similar fate befell the Second Secretary in Halle: he had "failed to organise the defence of Party Headquarters". Even the First Secretary at Goerlitz, Comrade Weichold, was dismissed. In spite of serious injuries at the hands of the demon-strators, he was found guilty of "capitulationism". The quasi-criminal courts remained in session for more than a year.

Meanwhile the first vague rumours of bitter disputes within

the Politbureau and the Central Committee reached the lower levels of the Party. Ever since the "new course" had been de- clared, the position of the Party's strong man, Walter Ulbricht, had seemed insecure. There was much speculation about a struggle for power; the Soviet High Commissioner, Vladimir Semyonov was said to have directed searing criticism at members of the Politbureau. There was no time to wait for interesting developments at the top, however. The SED had to act. It was decided that the Party's principal speakers should tour the factories, lead "open discussions" and simultaneously criticise both the strikers and themselves. It was announced that in the "struggle for the souls of the workers" the Party had "lost contact with the masses"; an attempt at reconciliation was to be combined with the campaign of vengeance being waged by the Security Service. Everybody of rank or note was pressed into the crusade. *Kuba*, a poet (the nom-de-plume derives from the plebean Kurt Bartels), set the tone in a leaflet addressed to the Stalinallee building workers. Its title announced that he was ashamed—not, he explained in the first verse, because they had marched but because they had marched in bad company, trotting after "international incendiaries and louts". Kuba re- minded them that "the good carpenter, Walter Ulbricht," had removed all their grounds for complaint (in the "new course") before they set out. He assured them that they could go to bed like good children at 9 o'clock, since the Soviet Army and the Comrades of the People's Police were guarding their sleep and World Peace. He suggested, as a former building-worker himself, that because the war-mongers' "X-Day" had come to naught, many more building-workers in the Democratic Republic would have the opportunity to become architects, painters, composers and poets. Finally, he asked whether they were not as ashamed as he was.

The building-workers were not ashamed. Nor did they want to be composers, painters and poets. They wanted reasonable wages, good food and freedom. And they found Kuba's effusions intensely irritating—he had in fact produced a classic example of what Marxism calls "loss of class-conciousness". Every one of the Communist leaders rediscovered his working-class origins in the weeks following the insurrection. But the men on the scaffolding and at the machines were not interested; the myth of the Workers' Party and Workers' Government had been shown up for what it was and the antics of Ministers, Secretaries of State, trades union leaders, newspaper editors and Party poets did nothing to repair the façade. The SED met with increased resistance; only 2,500 of the 28,000 men and women at the Leuna works crowded round the "good carpenter", Ulbricht, who had come with an escort of heavily armed People's Police to read them a lesson. In the discussion that followed, Ulbricht learned that times had changed. An engineer put the men's case in a few words. "If I make a mistake," he said, "I end up in prison. If the Government makes mistakes...?" Ulbricht discovered that Party men who had recovered their buoyancy were receiving parcels in the mail containing a length of rope and a scrap of soap. He learned that a remarkable amount of rejects were being produced and that output had dropped considerably. The Red Army newspaper, *Taegliche Rundschau*, reported that the Stalinallee building-workers had been "hurling abuse" at senior officials sent to reason with them. Passive resistance grew. The slogan "Work slower!" was passed round the factories and nobody bothered to whisper. Even in the coal mines at Zwickau, where no organised strike had taken place on June 17, output fell steeply; according to the Party Press the men at the coal-face were constantly found "doing nothing, and even asleep", and made insolent and improbable excuses when challenged.

Open resistance flared up repeatedly. At the dye-stuffs fac-tory at Wolfen the men went on strike on July 10 because the management refused to grant strike pay for June 17. Here and in a hundred other factories the workers answered their trade union officials with organised refusal to pay membership dues. In the Buna works, the SED's chief ideologist, Fred Oelsner, announced in a speech that X-Day would never be repeated. The men yelled back, "X-Day will come again!" This was on July 26. On July 15 the men had declared a sit-down strike. A few days earlier a committee had addressed a list of 29 demands to the Russian management and to the Government in Berlin; it was rejected as "the work of provocateurs". The men stopped work, threw Party officials out of the workshops and chased off a squad of People's Police who had arrived with fire hoses. They struck again next day.

In the Zeiss factory at Jena the State Security Service had avenged the rising, as everywhere else, with a series of arbitrary arrests. Among the men carried off was one Eckhardt Norkus, according to the management a "fascist and imperialist agent". The management added that the arrested man was a nephew of one Herbert Norkus, who had been killed in a fight with Communists in the 1930's and who became a Nazi martyr. This was sufficient to "expose" Eckhardt Norkus as a "fascist provocateur", and a Gera court sent him to prison for three years. On July 7 the news of the sentence reached the Zeiss factory and 1,500 men signed a petition demanding Eckhardt's release, and the release within three days of every striker against whom a criminal charge could not be proved. On July 9, at a union meeting on the factory premises attended by a thousand men, the chairman of the metal-workers' union, Hans Schmidt, wearily defended the regime. In dead silence the men heard him out; then one of them jumped onto the platform, presented the petition and spoke at some length about Norkus. The applause lasted several minutes and unrest continued for two days.

The SED leaders journeyed tirelessly, offering "trust in ex-change for trust" and finding no takers. Their tone became harsher and their audiences a wall of sullen, obstinate silence. Sometimes the workers spat out the truth to their faces, knowing that they would be "exposed as provocateurs" and that the political police were likely to be waiting at the factory gates. On June 17 the men had been together in their hundreds and thousands; now everyone acted and spoke alone—the courage and integrity of these men deserves deep respect. Whatever the workers said to the Communist bosses, all must have echoed the remark of a man named Bremse who stood up in front of Rudolf Herrnstadt, editor-in-chief of the central Party organ, *Neues Deutschland,* and a member of the Politbureau, at a mass meeting in the Siemens-Plania works in East Berlin on June 23, and said: "I am proud of the seventeenth of June!" Herrnstadt wrote in his newspaper that this "colleague Bremse" had said a terrible thing; but he scolded him in terms that were remarkably mild. It seemed that Bremse's pride, and above all the event of which he was so proud, had made a deep impression on Herrnstadt.

The Editor's personal concern with the errors of the Party, at the browbeating of the industrial worker and with the "new course" was evident not only between the lines of *Neues Deutschland* but in them. There were signs that Herrnstadt was using his position as the Party's chief publicist to support a movement within the Politbureau against Walter Ulbricht and his fellow exponents of a "tough" policy. Little was heard of the Secretary-General of the Party in those weeks; day after day people in the Soviet Zone and the West waited for the announcement which would confirm his downfall. The Government gave out repeated assurances that the "new course" would continue—Ulbricht's prospects, then, were surely poor. But the news never came. The Party Press promised that pro-vision would soon be made for "a more richly laid table and a fuller wardrobe", and announced that the pace of develop-ment of heavy industry would be reduced accordingly—for example, the number of blast furnaces at Stalinstadt would not now be increased from six to eight. Selbmann, Minister for Foundry Construction, announced that the output of pig-iron at Stalinstadt alone was double the entire previous national production of this commodity and that the output of the combined foundries was four times that of 1950; this, he said, justified a reduction in the Plan for heavy industry of 1.4 mil-liard marks. Heinrich Rau, Chief Economic Planner, made another 2 milliard marks available to invigorate the consumer goods industry, private industry and for agricultural credits. Food was released from the national reserves. People's Police stores were thrown open: 800,000 pairs of boots, 3 million square metres of woollens, 2 million pairs of socks, trousers and underpants, 100,000 bicycles and 13,000 motor-cycles were thrown onto the market. It was not much, but it was enough to whet the appetite for things to buy. In July the Government raised the wages of lower-paid workers by an average of a penny an hour, fulfilling a promise made a year before and departing from the policy of pegging low wages and raising the higher salaries in a steep curve. The Government emphasised that the workers had the (State) trades union movement to thank for this bounty; an effort was being made to earn a little credit for the whippers-in. Almost simultaneously certain prices were reduced: rice, tea, chocolate substitute, soap, women's stockings, electric light bulbs and typewriters became cheaper. A number of confiscated factories, shops and farms were returned to their owners; dismissed teachers and expelled students returned to schools and universities.

Otto Nuschke, leader of the bourgeois fellow-travellers, summoned up new courage and fathered the slogan "butter, not guns"; while the Soviet High Commissioner certainly took trouble in those weeks to breathe a little spirit of independence into the decimated and languishing ranks of the Christian Democratic and Liberal Democratic Party leaders. Primed with second-hand strength, Nuschke expressed a wish for a liberal economic policy and for legality and justice. And Prime Minister Grotewohl announced the release from goal of 7,800 people who had been arrested or sentenced for "economic crimes". He omitted, of course, to mention that the empty cells had been filled with strikers and demonstrators; nor did he say that not one of the thousands of men and women imprisoned for political resistance had been freed. In spite of an astounding display of soothing gestures, nothing fundamental had changed.

And yet the grip of fear had been broken and heads no longer hung. The seventeenth of June had left a breeze of freedom in the land. And freedom is contagious. Hardly noticeable at first, it spread into the all but impenetrable cadres of the Party. The young theorist, Wolfgang Harich, Professor of Marxism-Leninism at the East Berlin University, published a violent attack on the "high priests of the State Commission for Cultural affairs" and lashed the official literary critics for obstructing the progress of science and the arts with their "disgraceful political belittling", their "shocking dilettantism" and their "misuse of German artists by urging them to adopt purely national features of Russian realism". Harich also assailed the "bureaucratic and mechanical" jargon of the Party Press, complaining that it "hampered understanding between the two halves of Germany". Bertold Brecht, genius of the nineteen-twenties and the Soviet Zone's single literary lion, gave public utterance to some careful thoughts about "Socialist Realism", with its heroes at the tractor, lathe and shooting range. Should not Socialist Realism, with its "constructive humour" and "optimistic tragedies", he asked, be "critical realism" too? In other words, should not Bertold Brecht—whom membership of the activist-heroes-by-the-dozen school had not cured of a morbid fascination for the rotting corpse of decadent and bourgeois culture—also be accorded his rights? The "Cultural Federation" led by the Party bard, Johannes R. Becher, felt sufficiently rejuvenated to issue a fourteen-point memorandum asking for "freedom of opinion", and "an end of interference in creative affairs by administrative departments of State, a transformation of the style and contents of newspapers and radio programmes", "importation of technical literature from Western Germany and abroad", "independence of teachers", "freedom of discretion for writers, journalists, publishers, artists and producers"—in short, the satisfaction of all the natural aspirations and desires which the Party ideologist had tried so hard to persuade the hostile intellectual to forget. These truly revolutionary advances were beaten off; the rebellious Harich was accused of trying to liquidate all hard-won successes. On the other hand, a bridge-head for free discussion seemed to have been secured at last.

The herd of Comrades staggered from one shock to another, helping themselves as best they could with renewed excesses of contrition, confession, self-accusation and counter-accusation, begging for general absolution—this at least could not be wrong! Bertold Brecht, who had published an obsequious address of fidelity to the regime within a few hours of the collapse of the rising, jeered: "Despite most zealous reflection, they could not recall the nature of their mistakes; passionately, however, they claimed to have made them—as is the custom."

After the sharp reaction of the people to the conciliatory gestures of the "new course", the Soviet authorities in Germany might have been expected to order a return to the policy of the clenched fist. Nothing of the sort occurred. Though the centres of resistance were combed out ruthlessly, the new policy continued undisturbed. Clearly such a decision had not been made at Karlshorst but in Moscow, where signs of a new approach to internal and external affairs were now becoming frequent. The great experiment, however, was to be staged where the process of Sovietisation of society and economy had not been completed, where conditions were still variable, and where the political leaders had retained a measure of tactical flexibility. Hungary was the second of the satellites to adopt the "new course". The Hungarian Ulbricht, Matyas Rakosi, withdrew from the Government (keeping his commanding position as First Secretary of the Party); the pace of agricultural collec⁄ tivisation slowed down; the development of heavy industry relaxed; the resettlement of (largely Jewish) citizens of big towns was curtailed and a number of concentration camps were closed.

The oppressed peoples of Eastern and Central Europe, the populations of the Soviet Union and the peoples of the West began to take hope; if the rulers in the Kremlin were at last preparing to grant their millions of subjects some alleviation of material hardships, then surely they must favour some relax⁄ ation of international tension and must limit their gigantic armaments drive to free their resources to meet the demands of a peacetime economy. Sentiments such as these were evident in the speeches of the great elder statesman, Sir Winston Churchill.

On Friday, July 10, 1953, an alarming item of news from Moscow raced round the globe: Lavrenti P. Beria had been dismissed from his posts of Deputy Prime Minister and Minis⁄ ter of the Interior and his case had been handed over to the Supreme Court for consideration. The third man in the trium⁄ virate of Stalin's heirs had been overthrown—four months and four days after the dictator's death.

Discussion of the possible consequences of this grim sensation preoccupied the world for weeks. Would the Soviet Empire be plunged into another bloody purge on the Stalinist pattern; would its new leaders and the great Party itself go under in a struggle for power; would the Army intervene and attempt to set up a "Bonapartist" regime? Would the downfall of the Chief of Secret Police lead to the collapse of the secret police system itself? Above all, would the "new look" in internal and external affairs now be abandoned? Once again the free island of Berlin provided the Western observer with the opportunity to collect vital clues. For the eastern half of the city, the Party was still engaged in anxious discussion of the "lessons of June 17".

On July 9, *Neues Deutschland* had published a contributor's suggestion that it was not enough to "expose provocateurs" and that it might be more profitable to concentrate on "our mistakes as a political party". Editorial comment was more cautious; the writer warned against underestimating the "strength and cunning of the fascist underground", but stressed the "enormous significance" of the character of June 17 and spoke of the working class having been "misled" by elements who sought to exploit demands that were "justified but could not be fulfilled at this stage". They were careful words which showed that no one was yet prepared to commit himself to a firm line, that arguments were perhaps still raging in the Polit-bureau and Central Committee of the Party, and that it might be more prudent to await the return of the Soviet High Commissioner from a meeting in Moscow. The news of Beria's fall came next day. Two days later *Neues Deutschland* startled its readers with a change of tone. A leading article addressed to the "weak-kneed" declared that the "new course" and seven-teenth of June had given some Comrades the impression that the Party made nothing but mistakes. The Party organ now complained strongly of pessimism and undue desire to atone, and asserted that the "general line" had been substantially correct. The article might well have been penned by Ulbricht. Two days later Comrade Albert Hengst, a member of the Secretariat of the Central Committee, was expelled from the

Party for "capitulationism and support of provocateurs", while the Minister for Road Transport and Agricultural Machinery Construction, Bernd Weinberger, was severely reprimanded. (Both had been sent to the Baltic coastal area on June 17 and had shown insufficient energy in dealing with the strikers.) On July 16 the Minister of Justice, Max Fechner—with Grotewohl, the sole remaining ex-Social-Democrat in the Government and the Politbureau,—was dismissed. Fechner was charged with "activity hostile to the Republic" and the nature of his crime was self-evident. A fortnight earlier he had told a reporter that unjustifiable arrests had taken place since the rising; membership of a strike committee was not in itself an offence, he had said, and even suspected "ringleadership" was not enough to justify a sentence in the courts. He had cited as an example the case of a miner who had been acquitted by the district court in Frankfurt-on-Oder after evidence had been accepted that he had stood up at a meeting on June 17, and shouted that all strike-breakers were traitors to the working class. In a subsequent issue, *Neues Deutschland* had supplemented the interview with a number of remarks by the Minister which had been left out of the original version "owing to a technical error". The addendum stated in black and white: "The right to strike is guaranteed in the Constitution". Fechner was arrested and his successor, the vice-President of the Supreme Court and most hated and feared woman in Germany, Hilde Benjamin, promptly announced that the account with the provocateurs would now be paid in full. An official announcement followed: "From July 24 to July 26, the Central Committee of the SED met in Berlin under the chairmanship of Comrade Otto Grotewohl. The Central

Committee unanimously decided that as an enemy of Party and State, Fechner be dismissed from the ranks of the SED. It was further unanimously decided that Comrades Zaisser and Herrnstadt be dismissed from the Central Committee." The communiqué explained that the two men had formed a "hostile and defeatist faction" which had "set itself against the unity of the Party". The struggle for power was over and Ulbricht had won.

It transpired that Ulbricht's was a narrow victory; indeed he and his supporters had barely avoided disaster. Step by step the Minister of State Security had forced his confident way into the foreground. A school teacher and an ex-officer of middle-class background, Zaisser had found his way to the Communists after the first World War. He always preferred secrecy, joining the Soviet secret service early in his career and establishing himself as a trusted and effective organiser during the Ruhr riots, in the formation of the Party's military wing and later as military adviser to the Communist Party in China. For a brief period he became famous—as "General Gomez", Chief of Staff of the International Brigade in the Spanish Civil War. During the second World War the Russians chose to introduce Zaisser as the former leader of German *Stahlhelm* members in China to the officer prisoners-of-war of the "Free German National Committee"; he is also believed to have been one of the few Germans who commanded a Red Army unit in battle. Zaisser returned home with the conquerors and for a time remained in subordinate posts (he resumed his career in Germany as Chief of Police in Dresden). His chance came with the recruiting of military cadres for the People's Police and he was entrusted with their command.

In 1950 he founded the East German Ministry of State Security and assumed control of the political police force which had been nurtured at provincial level by representatives of the Soviet M.V.D. since 1946. Although the new Ministry was under direct Russian control—several Soviet "advisers" were attached to each provincial SSD office as well as to headquarters in Berlin—Zaisser soon acquired enormous power. It was the power of brutality and terror wielded by the master of all secrets; no event in however obscure a corner of the administrative machine and no development in the Party could remain hidden from the chief of the SSD. Zaisser was careful and patient; over the years he had learned to wait.

Rudolf Herrnstadt, too, returned to Germany from Moscow in 1945. The son of a Jewish lawyer from Silesia, he became a talented journalist and a secret member of the Communist Party. The liberal *Berliner Tageblatt* sent Herrnstadt to Moscow where he moved in diplomatic circles, serving his editors in Berlin and his contacts in the NKVD with equal skill. During the war he edited a nationalistbolshevik newspaper, *Neues Deutschland*, which circulated among German prisonersofwar in Russia; in 1945 he edited the nominally nonparty *Berliner Zeitung;* later he took over the Party's central organ, the by now frankly Communist *Neues Deutschland*. Herrnstadt was a writer; unlike the turgid and incomprehensible mouthings of his agitator colleagues, Herrnstadt's articles had style and bore the stamp of an agile and often mischievous mind. The masterpropagandist soon took his place as a Red Goebbels in the Central Committee of the SED and later became "candidatemember" of the Politbureau. He climbed adroitly and, as it seemed, lightfootedly, though he frequently came into open ideological conflict with Fred Oelsner, the favoured right-hand man of Walter Ulbricht. In Herrnstadt Zaisser found a popular partner, a man who could have influenced the masses and who commanded powerful support in the Party.

With the declaration of the "new course", the two men prepared their bid for leadership. Towards the end of July the text of Ulbricht's speech to the fifteenth Conference of the Central Committee reached West Berlin; this document and the polemics in the newspapers against Zaisser and Herrnstadt revealed a complex political intrigue whose roots extended beyond Berlin to Moscow. It was officially admitted that shortly after June 17 the Politbureau had set up a committee which then had recommended that Herrnstadt replace Ulbricht as First Secretary of the Party. A few days later Herrnstadt put to the Politbureau a draft resolution demanding a radical overhaul of the Party's leadership, organisation and character. "Were the Party to take the rights and interests of other social classes into account... we should receive the full support of all sections of the populace, including that of the working class," it said. In its economic provisions the resolution called for a strongly liberal trend—a trend, the Party judges found, which "would have led to a restoration of capitalism". That much was published for the benefit of Party members. Behind the doors of the Central Committee Ulbricht was more specific. He accused Zaisser of conspiring with Franz Dahlem, who had been expelled from the inner councils of the Party after the trial of the Czech Communist leader, Rudolf Slansky, in 1952; he alleged that Zaisser had planned to take over the Ministry of the Interior in addition to the SSD; and that Zaisser had negotiated to this purpose with two special emissaries sent from Moscow by Beria. Ulbricht added: "Zaisser's attitude corresponds with that of Beria, which is in turn associated with the ideas put forward by Churchill."

There are strong indications that Zaisser and Herrnstadt were proposing to dissolve the SED; to re-form the Communist Party and to create a left-wing Socialist Party on the lines of the Nenni Socialist group in Italy; to permit genuine rivalry with the centre parties and to return sizeable sections of industry to private ownership—in a sentence, they proposed to turn the East German Republic into a democracy. Such a course would make sense when seen as part of an overall plan for German reunification at the price of neutrality. Zaisser and Herrnstadt had not ceased to be Communists and passionate advocates of Soviet expansion. They were merely facing the fact that present policy was leading nowhere, that it was driving the Federal Republic towards West European integration and the population of the Soviet Zone into bitter hatred of Soviet Russia and the SED. However, such a far-reaching revision of Communist foreign policy could only have been drawn up at the summit—that is by Beria and his staff. The Praesidium of the Supreme Soviet had accused the former Minister of the Interior of attempting to place his department above Party and Government; the East German Central Committee accused Zaisser of attempting to secure control of the Ministry of the Interior, of trying to withdraw his Ministry of State Security from control by the Party, and of attempting to control the Party through the SDD. Beria was accused of secret designs which would have led to a restoration of capitalism (the same deadly sin was ascribed to Zaisser and Herrnstadt). Beria was further condemned for "undermining collectivisation" and for his liberal policy towards the minority nationalities. The official indictment said nothing about his foreign political plans.

There is no doubt that Beria's downfall obstructed the seizure of power in Berlin by the Zaisser-Herrnstadt group. At the same time it may well be true that the seventeenth of June in Germany contributed largely to the police chief's liquidation. His chief judge was Marshal Koniev. Shortly after Stalin's death, Marshal Zhukov, conqueror of Germany, returned from obscurity in Odessa to the post of Deputy Defence Minister— a stepping-stone, as it turned out, to further promotion. These and other facts indicate that the victor in the struggle against Beria's department was the Red Army; that the Generals lent their strength to Malenkov and Molotov; that the Army was interested in Beria's disappearance. What were the Generals' motives? Dislike of a police force with its own heavily armed élite formations and with powers of supervision extending into the regular army was probably their principal motive. But there is reason to believe that the seventeenth of June had alarmed the military leaders considerably. Political relaxation had caused the embers of passive resistance to burst into the flames of open rebellion. The intervention of the Soviet advanced western army had been required and for weeks the industrial centres had had to be guarded to prevent fresh disorders. It was in no sense a trial of strength, but major military formations had been tied down for weeks on end. Strikes and demonstrations had taken place in some 350 towns and villages of the Soviet Zone; it was found necessary to march Soviet troops into 150 of them. A handful of infantrymen had sufficed in many of the country districts; East Berlin, however, had required a fully equipped armoured division and a second was in reserve on the outskirts. Brandenburg, Magdeburg, Halle, Bitterfeld, Leipzig, Goerlitz, the uranium area of the south and the Baltic ports in the north—infantry and armoured units had been moved to all these widely separated points; at the western and eastern frontiers—though in fact there was no threat of infiltration either from the Federal Republic or from Poland—existing security measures had been augmented. It is true that a decision in Moscow or at Karlshorst to quench the rising in a bloodbath would have saved the use of troops on such a massive scale. On the other hand, organisers of an insurrection (had there been any) would not have been concerned in the first stages to mobilise the masses and send them on the streets. Using picked fighters, they would have attacked such key targets as powerstations, post offices, bridges, railways and trunk roads. A repetition of the rising—so the Russian military staffs might have concluded—could only be planned to take place on the outbreak of war; in this event the Germans, who had proved themselves capable of open resistance without weapons, would presumably be armed. The Red Army planners, then, were forced to consider a factor whose full implications only become apparent when we recall that since the war Polish partisans have been unceasingly active along the extended Russian lines of communication to central Europe; that the Poles would not hesitate to rise against their oppressors in the event of war; and that the Czechs and Hungarians might well follow their example. The vast rear area of the advanced Soviet armies might be faced with rebellion on a scale beyond the powers of local satellite armies to suppress; large Red Army formations might be tied down as parts of Hitler's *Wehrmacht* had been tied down by partisans in Soviet Russia. To continue the possible analysis of the Soviet General Staff, the course set by Beria might have put the Red Army in Europe in an un/ tenable position. And if the policy of freeing the Soviet Zone in exchange for a reunited, neutral Germany (with the prospect of later reconquest) had been successful, and the Soviet occu/ pation force withdrawn beyond the Polish frontier, would not the Poles, Czechs, Hungarians, Bulgarians and Rumanians have regarded such a decision as the beginning of the end of the Soviet empire, and would they not have followed the Germans' example of June 17?

At this point the bitter question arises whether the June rising did not destroy or at least postpone for a long period all opportunity of the East German people regaining their freedom. Today, more than two years later, the question is no easier to answer than it was in the anxious weeks which followed the seventeenth of June. Certainly the East German rulers have given no sign of learning anything from the rising; on the other hand, the people of the Soviet Zone are undemoralised and regard the rulers with unchanged revulsion. The people are aware that the rising influenced international developments— that the Western Powers' acceptance of the need for German reunification is in no small measure due to their efforts to bring it about themselves. The "new course" did not last and life in the Soviet Zone is little less grim today than it was two years ago. Nevertheless recent events have stimulated hope. While there is anxiety lest the Four Powers should agree to "solve" the German problem on the basis of the *status quo*, there is a feeling that unity may be approaching. The Soviet leaders' abject pilgrimage to Belgrade, Russia's signature of an Aus/ trian Treaty and above all the recent visit of the Federal

Chancellor, Dr Adenauer, to Moscow, are regarded as confirmation of an impression which even the intervention of Red
Army tanks on June 17 did not destroy—namely that Moscow's
policy is not entirely inflexible and that the Russians have
always avoided indentifying themselves with the Ulbricht-
Grotewohl regime. The German Communist leaders have for
their part now admitted that their policies are based on the
assumption that Germany will remain divided. On the eve of
the Geneva conference Premier Grotewohl declared that the
inclusion of the two German States in a European security pact
would reduce tension. It is obvious enough that only a
"solution" which perpetuated the *status quo* would enable the
Communist Government of Eastern Germany to survive; since
the 1953 rising its leaders policy has been directed to this end.

The Government's departure from the "new course" began
while Malenkov was still in apparent control in Moscow;
with Malenkov's replacement by Bulganin and Khrushchev
the wheel was turned full circle. During the Malenkov
phase, Fred Oelsner, the SED's principal guardian of true
Marxism, complained loudly that many prominent officials
were showing insufficient interest in the Marxist theory of
production. Lecturing on "The transition period from Capitalism to Socialism in the German Democratic Republic",
Oelsner revived all the old arguments in favour of priority for
heavy industry—referring at the same time to "distinctive
features of the German development of Socialism". He was
deliberately departing from the current Moscow line; he was
following Khrushchev. Somewhat surprisingly he declared that
since the new order in the German Democratic Republic had
sprung from the destruction of the imperialist order by the Soviet

Army, it could not be the outcome of a popular democratic revolution by the working class. Then he went on to say, "Since Germany was highly industrialised many years before the transitional period from Capitalism to Socialism began, there can be no question of applying in Germany the phase of industrialisation required in other countries." This was virtu-ally an admission that the East German economic order was not the result of any innate contradictions of the Capitalist society as prophesied by Karl Marx but was an artificial product of the Soviet Union's strategic requirements. Oelsner's remarks also indicated that the German Communist leaders no longer intended that production of consumer goods should continue at the high rate prescribed by the "new course". Ominously, Oelsner concluded his lecture with the warning that workers must not only fulfill their norms but must "somewhat exceed" them.

Fred Oelsner's lecture sealed the fate of the "new course". The Government renewed the campaign to raise the norms— not in the crude and brutal style of the weeks which preceded June 17 but nevertheless with much of the old, irresistible pressure. The policy which had turned sugar and butter into high-priced rarities had returned. But the constant agitation for higher productivity fell on deaf ears. Not only did output in almost all branches of industry remain at a low level, but the Government suffered defeat in its efforts to revive heavy industry. To take a single example from an official announce-ment made in the middle of 1955: more than seventy per cent of the total output of the Soviet Zone's iron-foundries had to be rejected as below the absolute minimum standard, with the result that important Soviet orders could not be met. Though the Marxist economic theorists racked their brains to discover how the Communist methods of total planning could be made to achieve the results they enviously observed in the Federal Republic, the economy they had fashioned according to the requirements of Russia hobbled from one bottleneck to the next.

The Communist leaders were able to claim some success in the field of "defending the achievements of the Workers' and Peasants' State". Soon after the rising the Government organised the recruiting of what were variously called "factory fighting groups" and "works' defence units". Scarcely troubling to disguise its fear of a repetition of the events of June 17, the Government announced that such units must be raised and trained in all nationalised undertakings for defence against "provocations by imperialist enemies". The factory fighting groups are manned by workers and students selected for their reliability. Each unit numbers ten men and is commanded by a "tactical group-leader"—generally an officer of the barrack-based People's Police—and by a "political group-leader", who is nominated by the Party organisation in the factory concerned.

The June rising and the demands of Soviet foreign policy compelled the East German leaders to step up recruiting for their barely camouflaged national army, the barrack-based People's Police. At first the recruiting officers relied on good-natured persuasion. The results were poor. They reverted to more energetic, trusted measures. The results were disastrous. There were more 18- to 20-year-olds in the refugee camps of West Berlin than in the barracks of the Soviet Zone.

Apprentices were threatened with expulsion and students with the withdrawal of scholarships; the delights of military service under "Socialism" were described in glowing terms.

But only a minority obeyed the call. Finally, even the SED newspaper, *Neues Deutschland*, conceded that all was not well, complaining of serious errors in recruiting policy. Admitting that "harmful methods" of recruiting were responsible for the "recent increase in persons deserting the Republic", the paper quoted what it described as an "isolated" example of a young Stralsund docker whose refusal to volunteer for military service was countered by threats of dismissal. The young man was also told that no other concern would be allowed to employ him. *Neues Deutschland* piously added that to threaten reluctant recruits with the sack, to cut their wages and stop their holidays was to depart from the principles of the Party. Perhaps because it was only too obvious that the number of genuine volunteers would not be sufficient to provide much more than an additional battalion, *Neues Deutschland* did not venture to propose an alternative to such measures, however.

The Soviet-organised Warsaw treaty organisation, if it is to be an effective counter-weight to NATO, must include a strong East German army. At the time of writing there is no conscription in the Soviet Zone. Yet the introduction of compulsory military service would do little to help matters—the passive opposition of the great majority of recruits would be hard for even the most dogged of Communist N.C.O.s to break down.

In these circumstances the Party has lately concentrated on converting the youngest children. In the spring of 1955 senior officials of the Young Pioneer organisation, which draws its members from the six- to fourteen-year-olds of either sex, were summoned to a conference and instructed in the arrangements for a major campaign to weaken family ties and to bring up the children as "Socialist patriots". An important feature of this campaign was the introduction of so-called "consecration cere-monies" for 14-year-olds on leaving school. After a ten-week course of instruction in Communist theory, with scientific and materialist explanation of the nature of the universe and the origins of Man, the children were required to take an oath to dedicate their lives to peace, progress and a number of in-nocuously phrased Communist aims. It was a new trial of strength for the Churches, whose leaders announced that Christian confirmation would be withheld from children who accepted the State's materialist substitute. Although both children and parents were subjected to considerable pressure— parents were visited in their homes by Party officials and school-children made to stand up in class and account for their reluctance to conform—the number of young people attending the ceremonies was surprisingly small. If Germany has to wait another five years for reunification, however, the regimentation of these children who are too young to have taken part in the 1953 rising will constitute a grave danger.

The Communists have had little success with the older children, particularly the students. An episode at the Univer-sity of Greifswald is worth relating as an example of the regime's failure to convert more than a minority of boys and girls who were not yet in their 'teens when the war ended. Early in 1955 the University was presented with a Government decree trans-forming the medical faculty into a military school of medicine directed by the barrack-based People's Police. The students rebelled; they called a strike and announced that they would attend no more lectures. For a short time the Government made no attempt to deal with this first effort at organised resistance by students; then the State Security Service moved into action. Many young men were imprisoned as "saboteurs" and a few managed to escape to West Berlin. But the strike continued. When reports of the medical students' courage reached the West, Swiss and Swedish students petitioned President Pieck on behalf of those who had been arrested. The spirit of the rising had not died.

It was alive at the Evangelical Congress at Leipzig in 1954, when 65,000 Protestants met to pray for reunification. Although not a "political" word was spoken, the underlying message of the speeches and sermons was clear to all. The occasion was a silent yet impressive demonstration against the totalitarian State and it gave to many renewed determination to hold out. This encouragement was badly needed; the Churches were already in the thick of a new struggle with the State. Church news-papers were being requisitioned, the Christian youth groups were once again being abused by the Communist Youth organ-isation, Church leaders were under heavy attack for their protests against the renewed anti-religious campaign. In theory the "new course" was still in force; it was simply being under-mined in easy stages.

Although the new rules which allowed freer travel between the two halves of Germany had been allowed to stand, fresh pin-pricks were directed at the long-suffering Western sectors of Berlin. For a time it seemed that the sudden imposition of greatly increased tolls for use of the *Autobahn* between Berlin and Western Germany might be the prelude to a new blockade. The Soviet High Commissioner gave the East German Govern-ment a free hand, rejecting his Western colleagues' protests with the assertion that the "Democratic Republic" was now

a sovereign State. They should negotiate with Herr Grotewohl, be suggested.

The Western Powers declined to grant the East German
Government implicit recognition, however. There is not the
slightest doubt that the German Communists have not been
able to recover the prestige they lost in June, 1953. But if the
regime's value to Moscow is questionable, the Russians cannot
afford not to give their creation every possible support. Molotov
and Mikoyan, Chou En-lai and, after the Geneva Conference,
even Bulganin and Khrushchev have visited East Berlin and
the Soviet Zone to demonstrate the high esteem in which Soviet Russia holds her German satellite. At each stage of the
German Federal Republic's advance in economic and political
influence and towards partnership in the Western community,
so the "Democratic Republic" has tried to show tangible
evidence of its pseudo-sovereignty. But Eastern Germany had as
yet been unable to rise above the status of a second-rate satellite.
The invitation to Federal Chancellor Adenauer to visit Moscow was a bitter blow to the East Berlin leaders; here was the
arch-enemy of Communist propaganda, about to be welcomed
by their own Comrades to the Communist mecca. The SED
leaders sought to diminish its effect with a new demonstration
of their own strength. At a rapid succession of show trials in
the summer of 1955 no less than six people were condemned
to death and executed as agents, spies and saboteurs. Walter
Ulbricht was proving to Moscow that he was a better German
than Konrad Adenauer, and the "Democratic Republic" a
worthier partner than the provisional Republic in Bonn.

CHAPTER XII

THE FACE OF REVOLUTION

*The strike under Communism ⁄ Collapse in East Berlin ⁄ Attempts
at leadership and organisation ⁄ Refuge in hope ⁄ National revolution
without nationalism ⁄ Revolutionary discipline ⁄ Why no intervention
from the West? ⁄ Volonté Générale ⁄ June 1953 and July 1944 ⁄ Role
of the individual ⁄ The classless revolution—on behalf of all Germany ⁄
Trust in Western Powers*

THE TITLE OF THIS BOOK REQUIRES SOME JUSTIFICATION.
"The East German Rising"—this is a precise description of
the occurrence which startled the world in June 1953. But was
it really a rising? Would it not be equally correct to speak of a
revolt, of a rebellion or of a revolution? Each of these expres-
sions has been used in the preceding chapters; each is relevant
and describes the character of events.

When the Stalinallee building-workers formed up to march
on June 16, they used a word which implied a clear and attain-
able objective—strike. It was the natural, legal weapon with
which the working class throughout the world had learned to
fight during the years of industrial development. Yet it is doubtful whether, at the moment of downing tools, many of the
building-workers realised the full implications of their action.
While the State trades union movent is, under the East German
Constitution, guaranteed the right to strike, little or nothing is
said about the conception of "State". The Communist regime
has repeatedly declared itself to be a "Workers' Government"
acting for an unopposed "Workers' Party" in a "Workers'

State". But this contention includes the claim that the demand of the working class for active partnership in the management of national affairs had found fulfilment with the seizure of power by the SED. It followed that any strike by the working class against the "Workers' Government" must be utterly absurd—indeed must be suicidal and criminal. A strike against Communist government anywhere is nothing less than open resistance to the State, is in fact a rising. Moreover, once this first step has been taken and the political order breached, two courses remain open: the striker either beats an immediate retreat, taking refuge in orthodox agreement with the conception of the "Workers' State" and in abject confession of an all but unforgivable aberration, or he goes on to the second step, with the Government's overthrow as his only possible objective. Half measures and semi-successes are out of the question; it is all or nothing. But if the concept of revolution can be applied to something more than the struggles of an already established ideology, if it can be applied, for example, to the enforced transfer of power from one political party to another, from one social class to the next—then the strike against a totalitarian State and its ruling class is in essence revolutionary.

The writer has tried to show that the strike of the Stalinallee building-workers found the East German Government in the classical position of the victim of revolution. The strike was perhaps only possible because the Government was ripe for overthrow. But the stoppage at Block 40 on the Stalinallee became the prologue of a revolutionary drama and the fact that the revolution was smothered while still at the stage of insurrection does not alter its character and objectives.

Like the absolute monarchy of the Kingdom of France on

the eve of the year 1789, like the more enlightened France of
Louis Philippe in 1848 and the princely houses of Germany;
like the Czarist Empire after the Japanese victories in 1905; like
Imperial Russia in 1917 and Imperial Germany in 1918—like
all these, the Soviet-German State was weak when the storm
of revolution broke loose. Revolutions presuppose the weakness
of States, whether they are encumbered by military defeats,
economic adversity or by a demoralised ruling class. Revolutions are never merely the reply to provocation. They are bear-
ers and executors of a belief in the need for a new and better
administration by new and better authorities. Revolutions are
creative. Whether they succeed or fail, they imply the defeat
of those they seek to overthrow, because they occur and because
they are possible. Thus each unsuccessful revolution leaves the
rulers with a suspended death sentence.

In the months which preceded June 17, the decline of power
in East Berlin became increasingly obvious. The Communist
leaders, pursuing their chosen course with feverish energy and
sweeping aside the realities that obstructed it, were disposed to
regard the growing harshness which their policy required as
evidence of their strength. It was nothing of the sort. Though
the capacity for punishment of the eighteen millions seemed
unlimited, their counter-pressure was mounting and would
perhaps have made itself felt sooner and more powerfully if it
had not been for the ever-present safety valve of the refugee
camps in West Berlin. How insistent this counter-pressure had
become was revealed when the monomaniacs in Berlin at last
saw themselves compelled to acknowledge their weakness in
going into reverse over the "new course". How the Government attempted to hold on to a last position in the matter of the

norms—and thus presented the tinder which caught the spark of revolution—has been described. The tinder flared, and the rest followed at breathless speed and with extraordinary precision. Twenty-four hours after a handful of men had downed tools, the entire Zone had risen. The strike required a demonstration and led to revolt. The first open clash of the rebels with authority required an appeal to the solidarity of the rest of the population and this was expressed in the demand for a general strike and for collective disobedience.

Strike, demonstration, revolt, rising... "rising" implied the attack of a movement without leaders or directions on the bastions of the regime; a one-hundredfold storming of the Bastille, of prisons, courts, headquarters of the political police, local government buildings and Party offices. And the rising was revolutionary in its objectives, for it sought the forcible overthrow of established authority and the seizure of executive and legislative power. There was not a factory or a town in which the Government's removal was not the cardinal demand. Because the government itself was out of reach, the rebels made do with those of its servants who fell into their hands. Everywhere there were attempts to organise the masses; throughout the Zone, strike committees were elected as a matter of course and a number of notable endeavours were made to form regional commands. In some places individual strike committees were combined in a central committee; perhaps the most advanced town in this respect was Goerlitz, where, before the assembled populace, the existing Town Council was declared removed from office and preparations made for its replacement by men who were able to claim that they represented a majority of citizens. A committee, led by a doctor and an architect and including delegates from larger factories in Goerlitz, was elected by acclamation. In Halle, an "Initiative Committee" tried to take over responsibility for affairs; in Bitterfeld, leadership was entrusted to a teacher, who found a place in his committee for representatives of all sections of the population, including the housewives. These are but a few examples; in the villages, too, mayors were deposed and revolutionary councils appointed to serve in their place.

A rising requires the masses, the closely knit ranks and the simple force of numbers. The masses in turn need the individual, the spokesman who can distil their feelings, turn their desires into demands and point the way to their fulfilment. But when the leaders had been chosen, what were they to suggest that would promise victory? What decisions were most likely to bring success?

Throughout the Zone the interval between action by the strikers and counteraction by the occupation force was brief, and often Soviet tanks had moved in before a small group of determined men had come forward to lead the rising. By then it was too late to strike at the most sensitive parts of the regime's nervous system. Only too seldom were key points attacked, as at Dresden where the strikers assaulted the main post office only to find an impenetrable cordon of troops and police barring the way. The authorities invariably secured such targets from the start; on the other hand, local government and Party offices, even prisons, were often surrendered without a struggle. The strikers' instinctive choice of the latter group of objectives must be deplored by the coolheaded strategist as a fatal error, for the Government's power was not anchored in the prisons and its position could scarcely be threatened by an army of under nourished political internees. Organisers of the rising—had there been any—would have given top priority to destruction of the police communications system and seizure of key road and railway junctions. The opening of the prisons they would have left as their last and crowning act. And yet it is just the inexperience, the dilettantism, the upsurge of a simple sense of justice and of human feeling which gives the June rising nobility.

For two, three, six and in some cases for twelve hours the working class marched in the intoxicating conviction of having snatched power from the regime. With sure instinct the re-volutionaries had sensed the Government's weakness; they had no doubt that the sudden switch to a "soft" policy had not been conceived in Berlin but in Moscow. They concluded that the occupation force would choose to sacrifice Ulbricht and his followers in order to ally itself with a majority of the people. And they felt encouraged in their hopes when they observed that local Red Army headquarters and garrisons were pointedly standing aloof. The rebels were not to know that they were being deceived by clever tactics—that the Red Army Commanders considered it essential to avoid any clash with the civil population until the order could be given for a blow so sudden and so massive that further resistance must seem futile. The disappointment, when the blow came, was bitter; hope of Russian sympathy had been great. Yet even in the matter of their attitude towards the Russians the strikers had shown shrewd political judgement. They were able to suppress their loathing of the foreign masters, and to stifle grim memories of murder, pillage and rape which had accompanied their "liber-ation"; in the heat of the struggle they called for prudence and enjoined one another to leave the Russians alone. Their intention was to elicit the neutrality, perhaps even the benevolent neutrality, of the occupation force; and in isolated instances they were not entirely unsuccessful, winning the sympathy of individual soldiers and inducing more than one Russian officer to betray calm indifference to the fate of the Ulbricht Govern, ment. The overwhelming majority of the strikers took immense pains to avoid giving the Red Army any reason to intervene; in the Soviet,owned Corporations it was never the Russian directors and managers, but always their German assistants, who were abused and belaboured. Not until the Soviet tanks bore down on them and Russian bullets cut into the crowds did the strikers give expression to their hatred of foreign domination and hurl stones, dirt and curses at the Soviet sol, diers. Every adolescent in the Soviet Zone of Germany knows that the source of misery is not in East Berlin but in Moscow, and that Ulbricht merely leads a band of obedient German stooges. The Russians met with undisguised hostility on June 17, but the people's cry for revenge was directed at the German quislings. The seventeenth of June was a national rising. But it was not a nationalist brawl: at no time were Russian soldiers exposed to the furore of nationalism. Nor were the demon, strators' passions aimed at the sons of Russia; they were hated not as Russians but as representatives of the Soviet State—of a foreign Power that had brought torment and distress into the land.

Their attitude towards the occupation force shows that the rebellious millions were prepared to submit to discipline. One might also, with admiration not unmixed with irony, regard as additional proof of the German sense of order the fact that the strikers leapt on any ruffian who attempted to steal private property, that they shied away from senseless destruction, that in the attacks on Party offices they almost invariably left furniture and equipment untouched and cleared out only paper. Stories from Bitterfeld have told how the strikers paused in the march through the town to break open refreshment booths and cook sausages; the column did not move on until every man had paid the proper sum and the total takings had been placed, together with a written statement, in the till.

In spite of examples of mob law and lynching, a search for signs of anarchy among the events of June 17 is unrewarding. Wherever the rebels were able to find trustworthy leaders, they submitted to their guidance unhesitatingly. The workers and citizens were not only out to capture power, they were eager to shoulder the responsibility that goes with it. Conscious of their own general discipline, the people thought they could induce the Russians to respect and legalise their demands. When these naïve hopes were dispelled by force of arms, they transferred them to the West, longing for the aid which alone could bring victory. Feverishly the strikers watched for signs of intervention by the American and British occupation forces. It was beyond their comprehension—and who shall blame them?—that the nations of the free world with whom they felt themselves allied, should stand idly by while the Soviet Union crushed the rising with its war machine. In some places rumour had it that American tanks had crossed the zonal border, that American aircraft were to drop weapons. Absurd as such expectations were, it would be unjust to condemn them too harshly. It could not have been easy, in that moment of acute disappointment, to remember that the Western Powers, in giving their active support to the rebels, would be taking upon themselves the risk of plunging the world into war. That there was simply no opportunity to deliver the eighteen millions from their hopeless isolation must have been regretted bitterly by everyone in the West—whether German, American, Briton or Frenchman—to whom professions of community with the oppressed peoples of Eastern Europe are more than empty propaganda. As Russian troops patrolled the streets that evening, many Soviet Zone Germans felt the distress of separation and loneliness more acutely than ever before. They may have recovered their breath sufficiently to be able to appreciate the impossibility of Western military intervention; but many felt that organisations in West Berlin or in Western Germany might at least have provided central leadership for the rising from outside. Some were inclined to regard this as the natural task of RIAS, the American radio station in Berlin—and so waited, in vain, for instructions, not realising that RIAS was limited as an organ of the American State Department to the provision of news, programmes and comment and was unable to take political action on behalf of the West. They had hoped, also, that West Berlin trades union leaders might take over the job of forming a central strike committee. But it was impossible; to have intervened would have been to lay the strikers open to subsequent prosecution as "traitors, acting for Western organisations". The Federal Ministry for all-German Affairs in Bonn adopted a policy of strict reserve for similar reasons.

The eighteen millions did not understand; were they not marching in order to tear down the barriers that divided their country and to take by storm the freedom which was being denied to them? To many it seemed a foregone conclusion that the Germans in the West would rise and join them; strikers who found asylum in West Berlin after June 17 repeatedly asked why their West German colleagues had failed to declare an immediate sympathy strike. They were rarely impressed by the reply that a strike in Western Germany would have harmed the national economy—that the strikers themselves would have borne the cost, that the working class in the Federal Republic had no sound reason to strike against either the employers, the Government or the occupation forces. To the men and women of the Soviet Zone it was not a question of striking "against" anything; it was a matter of striking "for" something —and "with" *them*. They longed for tangible evidence of sympathy and interest; words were not enough. It was not easy to explain that conditions in Western Germany were not such as to provide a ready tinder for their own revolutionary spark; nor is it possible to deny that interest in the Soviet Zone rising among people of Western Germany might well have been more lively. Whole-heartedly, the people of the Soviet Zone had put their trust in solidarity—how were they to understand that the mighty force which had united them in spontaneous revolution could stop at an artificial frontier?

Their solidarity explains the spontaneity of the rising; it also accounts for the speed with which the revolt swept from the Stalinallee in Berlin to 350 towns and villages of the Soviet Zone. Irrespective of origin, character, sex, social and profes-sional ties or age, millions of individuals acted as one, obeying the same signals, striving to reach the same goal and form-ulating the same programme: Rousseau's *volonté générale*, the sovereignty of the general will. The doctrine from which true democracy derives had come to Germany at last.

Attempts have been made to draw a distinction between the

two great and tragic days of German revolt against the modern totalitarian State—July 20, 1944 and June 17, 1953—by describing the first as "resistance" and the second as a rising. "June 17", it has been said, "was one of those simple eruptions which occur at intervals in history and which may or may not be of consequence... A rising takes place within the rudimentary sphere of politics; resistance, on the other hand, is a matter of ethics... A rising is concerned exclusively with unbearable aspects of the existing situation; resistance is determination to replace them with something better." It is right to interpret resistance as an ethical achievement. Certainly there can be no such thing as ethical achievement by the masses, only of individuals. But the argument ignores the fact that a rising requires the sum of the will to resist of the individuals taking part. The revolt against Hitler of July 20, 1944 was the act of an élite, of a few who were compelled to work in tragic isolation from the people. The anonymous élite of the revolt against the Communist State always knew itself to be in complete accord with the bulk of the population. But the objective in each case was the re-establishment of law, order and justice. The events of July 1944 and June 1953 have this in common: each called upon individual men and women who had been prepared for action by years of personal opposition and open or secret resistance.

Who were the men and women who "made" the June rising as members of strike committees and revolutionary councils? June 17 showed that despite the brief interval between the end of the Third Reich and the consolidation of Communist Government, the tradition of free socialism and independent trade unionism endures. Though forced underground, it is kept alive by those whose memories reached back to the Weimar

Republic. Many of the leaders on that day were veteran Social Democrats and staunch trade unionists. There were even old Communists among them, men who had reported for duty in 1945 after twelve years in Hitler's concentration camps and who had seen the betrayal of the working class by practical Communism. On June 17 they marched with the rest. The youngsters, too, were well to the fore; twelve years of Nazism and eight years of Communism had failed stifle to their individualism. Later, during the weeks and months of revenge for the seventeenth of June, the Party Press pursued the line that the rising was the work of "fascist bandits"; the inquisitors were able to produce evidence in a number of cases that convicted "provocateurs" had been members of the Nazi Party or of its subsidiary organisations, members of the SS, lesser leaders of the SA and Hitler Youth, or ex-officers and N.C.O.s of the *Wehrmacht*. Such disclosures, they believed, provided excellent material with which to discredit the rising. But the fact that former Nazis took part does not in itself make the rising National-socialist. The Hitler Youths, Nazi Party members and soldiers of a few years before marched for the same reasons as had everybody else. And how many Germans of between 25 and 35 years of age had escaped membership of the Hitler Youth? How many 20- to 50-year-olds had not served in some branch of Hitler's armed forces? It is true that several former officers and N.C.O.s played a leading part in local strike committees. The explanation is simple enough; they had learned to make rapid decisions and were practised in the technique of "getting things organised". On that day they showed that in addition to soldierly bravery they were equipped with the moral courage of responsible civilians.

The Communist leaders in East Berlin were not entirely uninformed when they stressed the participation in the rising of ex-soldiers. Otto Grotewohl himself showed unusual saga-city when he told the Central Committee of the S.E.D. that the composition of the working class had altered considerably since 1945 when, "in the course of democratising the machinery of State the best, most active, most faithful and most class-conscious elements" had been taken from the factories and given positions of responsibility in the administrative, economic and cultural branches of government. More specifically, Grote-wohl added: "160,000 factory workers became civil servants... at the same time several thousand fascists and members of the middle class—civil servants under the Nazi regime, or employers and businessmen who were opposed, or foreign to the new order—went into the factories as workers."

Thus had the "new Society" developed. Year after year the more obedient and ambitious Comrades were taken from the factory bench or from desks they had occupied as humble clerks, and put to work as officials of State and Party, as lecturers, managers, directors and magistrates. In their thousands they joined the ranks of a new ruling caste of privileged bureau-crats that stood in immutable opposition to the proletarian mass to which all other classes had been reduced. Thus it was that on June 17 the "classless society" became reality—though not in the form foretold. The Communists had succeeded in uniting all classes of the population against them. Working-men marched to prisons to liberate their employers; employees demanded that dispossessed owners of factories, shops and farms be given back their property and legal rights. They were not formulating a political programme, they were not calling

for the blessings of moderate capitalism and a free economy—
programmes and dogmas did not interest them. Nor were they
dreaming of the good old days of plenty. They had merely
learned the lesson well and thoroughly that a system which
destroys freedom brings distress and shortage in its place.

Historians have taught us to regard the French Revolution of
1789 as the rebellion of a liberal middle class spurred on by a
young industrial proletariat, and to interpret the upheavals
of the twentieth century as the rise to power of the Fourth
Estate. Gradually the theory of the "class character" of revolutions has come to be widely accepted; perhaps the concept of
the "classless revolution" will one day be regarded as dating
from June 1953.

The seventeenth of June might also be called the revolution
which did not aim at Utopia. Its first aim was expressed in
simple and moving terms by an elderly factory worker several
weeks before the storm broke: "We want to live like human
beings; that is all we ask!" he cried. No philosopher seduced
the masses with a shining vision of an ideal society and a
grandiose future. No ardent visionary offered them a "social
contract"; no lawyer offered a State fashioned according to the
principle of equal rights. No economist or sociologist persuaded
them to follow a carefully charted course leading to human
happiness, peace and universal welfare. No obscure conspira-
tor interpreted history for them; nobody foretold the future.
No Rousseau, Marx or Lenin had walked before them.

The authors of revolution in our epoch were never deeply
concerned with the present, with their contemporaries and
with their own surroundings. They thought and planned in a
distant future and sought to pierce its darkness with the search-

lights of their prophecy. The men of action who set about bringing their laws and plans to life in order to create the new world—the executors of revolutionary ideologies whom we have learned to fear as constructors of the modern totalitarian State—these, too, live and think in two of the three dimensions of time: in the future and in the past. It is absurdly true that the dictators, who never tire of boasting that they are realists, are least interested in the present. They plan, build, destroy and murder for the sake of "tomorrow"—never for "today". They claim to act for the sake of the ultimate perfection of the world, humanity and society. The march to a final resting-place, at which the survivors may settle down to enjoy questionable eternities, justifies for them every sacrifice, excuses the mounds of corpses they leave in their wake, and deafens them to the curses, sobs and entreaties of all they drive before them.

But on June 17 the people rose against the men who wanted to bring heaven down to earth and had in fact opened the gates of hell. Their revolution was concerned with the present and not the future, with the feasible and not the ultimately desirable, with life and not with ideologies. That is why the women of the country took part with a determination, courage and readiness to make sacrifices which equalled that of the men. A revolution which demanded daily bread instead of paper plans, which tried to rescue home, family and privacy from usurpation by the State—a revolution dedicated to the present and to the practical—had to be the affair of the women too. June 17 demanded legal rights, human dignity and, above all, freedom. It sought the oxygen without which life goes flat; it sought the room to move and manoeuvre which both genuine progress and the individual must have if they are not to suffocate.

In the long run the call for freedom would not in itself have sufficed as a substitute for a clear and sober definition of objec-tives; the need for a detailed programme would have become urgent in the first moment of victory. It is indeed quite possible that the revolutionaries' policies would not have tallied in every respect with those of the Federal Republic and the Western world. On the other hand it was not items in a programme which drove the people onto the streets; it was a common and elementary desire for freedom as the only state which guaran-tees a system of justice based on humanitarian principles. This fact should finally dispose of the suggestion that "the West has no message". The West has the message of freedom.

The June revolution was also concerned with the freedom of the nation, and with its right to reunite. It wanted to oblit-erate the defeats of 1945 and 1933 and sought a return to free German statehood. This was not a matter of revenge or nationalism, but of justice and legality. Thus it was a revolu-tion on behalf of all Germany, which may one day date its history from June 17, 1953, as France dates her modern history from July 14, 1789. The seventeenth of June sought a Germany which does not yet exist. The "German Democratic Repub-lic", whose end seemed to have come on that day, was never more than a shabby façade which failed to hide the distressing reality of a German province of the Soviet Empire. And it should not be forgotten that the Federal Republic is not Germany. There can be no Germany whose capital is not Berlin, which does not include Halle, Wittenberg, Breslau and Koenigsberg. Bonn can speak and act for Germans, because it is free. But Bonn is not the Germany whose life began in the jubilation and the torment of June 17. The conception of a State known as the Federal Republic functions; indeed it functions better than we dared hope, and we must be grateful for this, as the people of the Soviet Zone are grateful. But the Federal Republic was born of necessity. It is like a democracy generated in a test-tube; it can scarcely be cured of a grave deficiency disease, for a democratic State must be more than a functional machine. It does not need an ideology, but it does need its baptism of fire. Every modern democracy was born of revolution, of an outbreak of the "general will" in which the people saw itself to be sovereign. In recent years the Germans have met with devastating criticism of their history, based on the fact that there has never been a German revolution. The German revolution has now come about. It is not yet ended; nor can its victory be complete until the day of reunification dawns.

The German revolution began in the rising of June 17, with the march of the Stalinallee building-workers who—in the words of a French newspaper editor—"restored to Germany her dignity". On that day there occurred a "German miracle" which had nothing to do with economic recovery. The miracle convinced the world that the Germans do not only act on the orders of authority, but also against authority; it showed that they know how to fight not only under the spell of servitude but for freedom; not only with rifles and artillery but with bare fists and bounding heart, against the might of modern weapons. The world learned that the heart of this nation, too, can beat in freedom's cause. The seventeenth of June lifted a part of the dreadful load which Germans shouldered when they allowed themselves to be bewitched by totalitarianism. On the evening of June 17 a Jew of Polish-German origin—a man who had little reason to forgive and forget—said that this day had done more for Germany's rehabilitation than had all her achievements since the capitulation. This, too, is a product of the vicarious struggle and sacrifice of the eighteen millions. The people of the Federal Republic of Western Germany should be deeply grateful.

There remains the question whether the 1953 rising is now no more than a stirring memory, or whether that extraordinary event still exerts an influence on Soviet Zone developments. The answer is that the latter unquestionably holds true. The people of Eastern Germany would long ago have given up the struggle if it were not for the assurance the seventeenth of June has given them that the Communist leaders are not invincible— and if it were not for indications that the Soviet leaders are being careful to avoid committing themselves entirely to the existing regime. There is not the slightest doubt, however, that the will to oppose will die if the Western Powers should appear ready to accept the Soviet proposal of a European security system based on the present division of Germany—here it should be said that the insistence of the Western Powers, notably of Great Britain, at Geneva that there can be no European settle, ment without German reunification will not have passed un, noticed by a people whose confidence in the integrity of the Western nations has firm roots. But their resistance to Commun, ist oppression can only survive as long as they feel that German unity is not—or at least not only—a question of *strategic* importance to the West.

There will not be another East German rising. The indus, trial and office workers, the farmers and housewives who rebelled in 1953 know that a demonstration against the SED

Government today could only destroy the slim chances of regaining their freedom that remain. They place all their hopes in the Western Powers. A policy of appeasement is the last thing they want from the West. They ask for strength, courage and imagination. During the rising the people of the Soviet Zone waited in vain for help. Today they believe that the West is firmly on their side. These hopes should not be disappointed.